Once Saved, Always Saved.

A Biblical Defense Of Eternal Security.

Matthew Correll

Contents.

Preface.
1. God Cannot Lie.
2. What if someone stops believing?
3. Can salvation be given back?
4. OSAS and eternal life.
5. OSAS taught by Jesus.
6. And they shall never perish.
7. Sealed and Secure.
8. Assurance of salvation.
9. False Eternal Security.
10. What is faith concerning OSAS.
11. Problem Passages Explained.
12. OSAS And Sin.
13. OSAS And The Gospel.
14. Objections to OSAS.
15. Faith Is Not A Work.
16. OSAS and Greek Tenses.
17. OSAS and Suicide.
18. OSAS and Rewards.
19. OSAS and Evangelism.
20. OSAS and Church History.
21. OSAS and the Old Testament.
22. How To Defend Eternal Security.
Addendum.
My Doctrinal beliefs.

Preface.

What is eternal security? Eternal security is the biblical truth that God alone saves believers in Christ and thus keeps them forever saved by His infinite power. Nothing can alter, change, annul, cancel or cause salvific loss once a person is saved by the free grace of God.

Here is the definition from Robert L Dean Ministries:

1—Definition: the work of God which guarantees that God's free gift of salvation is eternal and cannot be lost, terminated, abrogated, nullified, or reversed by a thought, act, or change of belief in the person saved. Since man does nothing to earn or deserve the free gift of salvation, he can do nothing to lose the free gift of salvation. God does not give with strings attached; he does not take back what He once gives. Eternal security is defined as an unbreakable relationship with the integrity of God, the perfect righteousness, absolute justice, and immeasurable love of God. It is an unbreakable relationship because God will not break the relationship regardless of what we do or fail to do.

2—God the Father's purposes in salvation cannot be overridden. The same group He foreknew, He predestines, called, justifies and redeems. A careful examination of these verses shows that of those who are eventually glorified none are lost from those foreknown. Omniscience of God knows all the knowable, every contingency, possibility and permutation out to infinity. He perceives simultaneously, instantly, eternally, all the knowable. Foreknowledge is a subcategory of divine omniscience. In foreknowledge God distinguishes between the actual and possible and knows who of his creatures is positive at God consciousness and would respond to whatever impetus to be saved, and those who would not. God desires that all men be saved and so those who are foreknown are elect. In the divine plan set forth in the Divine Decrees God determined that in human history His sovereignty would coexist with human volition so that His will would not override or abrogate human responsibility. Unquote.

    This doctrine is true but only to those who have put their faith alone in Christ alone. They've trusted in what Jesus Christ has already done for them at Calvary. Namely that He died on the cross for their sins, was buried and rose again, making full atonement for sins, past, present and future which permanently secures the salvation of all who simply believe on Him. Hebrews 9:12. Job 11:18.

    My favorite verse in the whole Bible is an eternal security verse.

    John 6:47.

    Verily, verily, I say unto you, He that believeth on me hath everlasting life.

    This is Jesus Christ the Saviour of the world telling the believer that they are not only saved, but … Once saved, always saved. I hope you enjoy this presentation of the most important theological, soteriological truth, contained in God's Word. Here is the current gospel presentation I use to

evangelize.
    God bless.

How To Be Simply Saved.

1. **The bad News.** We are sinners. (Romans 3:23.) We deserve to be punished in hell for our sins.

2. **The Good News.** Jesus Christ who is God's Son died on the cross for all of your sins. He was buried & rose again to give you eternal life in heaven as a free gift. (1 Corinthians 15:3-4. Romans 6:23.)

3. **How am I saved?**
<u>Believe</u> on the Lord Jesus Christ and thou shalt be saved. (Acts 16:31.)

4. **Once saved, always saved.**
Jesus said in John 6:47. Verily, verily, I say unto you, He that believeth on me hath everlasting life.

Do you believe that you are saved by grace and promised heaven because Jesus died for you?
                  Yes_ No_.

1 – God Cannot Lie.

One of the main reasons why the believer in Christ is eternally secure is because of the nature and character of God. What God says stands forever true.

Psalm 119:160.

Thy word is true from the beginning: and every one of thy righteous judgments endureth for ever.

Psalm 89:34-35.

My covenant will I not break, nor alter the thing that is gone out of my lips. Once have I sworn by my holiness that I will not lie unto David.

God has made a covenant with all believers.

Genesis 17:7.

And I will establish my covenant between me and thee and thy seed after thee in their generations for an everlasting covenant, to be a God unto thee, and to thy seed after thee.

By faith alone Abraham was saved (declared righteous) Genesis 15:6. In verse 17:7 the seed is referring to believers and all believers are in an everlasting covenant. (Acts 3:25, Romans 4:16, Galatians 3:29.) A covenant that according to Psalm 89, God will not break. The reason why God will not break the covenant is because it is based on what He has sworn, namely that the one who believes on Jesus Christ has everlasting life. John 3:36. The only way someone could lose their salvation would be for God to go back on His word, but He cannot.

Psalm 89:35.

Once have I sworn by my holiness that I will not lie unto David.

God's word cannot be broken.

John 10:35.

If he called them gods, unto whom the word of God came, and the scripture cannot be broken.

The phrase "cannot be broken" literally means: is true forever.

Romans 3:3-4.

For what if some did not believe? shall their unbelief make the faith of God without effect? God forbid: yea, let God be true, but every man a liar; as it is written, That thou mightest be justified in thy sayings, and mightest overcome when thou art judged.

Men lie habitually; but God not only doesn't lie … He cannot lie. So therefore our eternal security is based on His immutable integrity and holy character. (1 Samuel 2:2, Revelation 15:4. Revelation 4:8.)

Titus 1:2.

In hope of eternal life, which God, that cannot lie, promised before the world began.

See eternal life was promised to the believer before anyone was ever born even before the world and life existed. It is true that one receives eternal life at the very moment they believe on Christ for it, John 3:16, but the very promise was made before anyone was even born proving that it is an unchangeable promise—and that nothing done in this lifetime can alter it.

So the idea of losing salvation is categorically preposterous in light of this verse. Look at the following verses.

Numbers 23:19-20.

God is not a man, that he should lie; neither the son of man, that he should repent: hath he said, and shall he not do it? or hath he spoken, and shall he not make it good? Behold, I have received commandment to bless: and he hath blessed; and I cannot reverse it.

If God were a man surely He would change His mind and reverse our salvation, but to prove that God is divine; He doesn't behave like fickle man. A saved person couldn't be lost again even if he wanted to because God cannot lie, break a promise or go back on His divine word.

Hebrews 6:18.

That by two immutable things, in which it was impossible for God to lie, we might have a strong consolation, who have fled for refuge to lay hold upon the hope set before us.

Salvation is based on a hope that is set before us. Jesus Christ already died for our sins and shed His blood for us. 1 Peter 1:18-19. Therefore the offer of eternal life is for everyone and given to all who believe the gospel promise. The simple fact that God already provided salvation for us proves eternal security because nothing in the future can negate what transpired in the past. (Ecclesiastes 3:15.)

The critics of this doctrine have not understood this concept. The bottom line is that our salvation is a free gift and has been settled in heaven. This is an important fact to note considering that heaven is a place of perfection and absolutely no sin. 2 Peter

3:13. Therefore what is settled in heaven is forever settled.

Psalm 119:89.

For ever, O L<small>ORD</small>, thy word is settled in heaven.

Psalm 119:138.

Thy testimonies that thou hast commanded are righteous and very faithful.

Psalm 110:4.

The L<small>ORD</small> hath sworn, and will not repent, Thou art a priest for ever after the order of Melchizedek.

Psalm 111:9.

He sent redemption unto his people: he hath commanded his covenant for ever: holy and reverend is his name.

God bless.

2- What If Someone Stops Believing?

This question comes up often when the doctrine of eternal security is discussed. The issue is of the believer that for whatever reason stops believing.

"Is he still saved?"

I've heard people say that they believed in eternal security but weren't sure if it applied to someone if they stopped believing. Some have said that the one who ceases to believe was never saved to begin with. But we must not opine or speculate based on man's wisdom. We must always turn to God's Word and see what it says.

Romans 3:3-4.

For what if some did not believe? shall their unbelief make the faith of God without effect? God forbid: yea, let God be true, but every man a liar; as it is written, That thou mightest be justified in thy sayings, and mightest overcome when thou art judged.

"For what if some did not believe?" This is referring to a saved person actually not believing any longer. So obviously this scenario does exist. But the Bible says that their unbelief cannot render the faith of God of none effect. We must remember that it is the faith of Jesus Christ, which is a perfect and unfailing faith that saves us. (Romans 3:22.)

Man may lose faith from time to time or even stop believing altogether due to ontological tragedy but this in no wise nullifies the perfect faith of Jesus

Christ or the work He did for us at the cross of Calvary. (John 19:30. John 17:1-5.)

Look at the following verses.

2 Timothy 2:11-13.

It is a faithful saying: For if we be dead with him, we shall also live with him: If we suffer, we shall also reign with him: if we deny him, he also will deny us: If we believe not, yet he abideth faithful: he cannot deny himself.

Verse 11 says if we be dead with Him. That is referring to being positionally associated with Christ and this is a permanent positional truth. Verse 12 is talking about suffering with Him which for those who do through perseverance and trials etc., they will reign with Christ and this is a reference to eternal rewards. When it says "He will deny us" it is referring to rewards or reigning with Christ not salvation. If we believe not He abides faithful. This means if we stop believing; God abides faithful and salvation is remains eternally secure.

We must never think that it is our faithfulness that saves us. Jesus said thy faith hath saved thee (Luke 7:50). Faith, a single passive act, not faithfulness. It is not our faithfulness that saves us but Jesus Christ, the faithful Saviour. (John 3:17. 1 Peter 4:19.)

God remains faithful even if and when we do not.

1 Corinthians 1:8-9.

Who shall also confirm you unto the end, that ye may be blameless in the day of our Lord Jesus Christ. God is faithful, by whom ye were called unto the fellowship of his Son Jesus Christ our Lord.

Conclusion: One is saved by grace alone

through faith alone in Christ alone and lack of faith or even a total departure of faith cannot alter the fact that we were saved. Nothing can. Romans 8:38-39. Once saved, always saved is true because God is forever faithful.

David the Psalmist completely understood this wondrous truth.

Psalm 121:1-8.

I will lift up mine eyes unto the hills, from whence cometh my help. My help cometh from the LORD, which made heaven and earth. He will not suffer thy foot to be moved: he that keepeth thee will not slumber. Behold, he that keepeth Israel shall neither slumber nor sleep. The LORD is thy keeper: the LORD is thy shade upon thy right hand. The sun shall not smite thee by day, nor the moon by night. The LORD shall preserve thee from all evil: he shall preserve thy soul. The LORD shall preserve thy going out and thy coming in from this time forth, and even for evermore.

For the sake of the argument, I'm not saying that all who turn their back on God and perhaps become a self-professed atheist or agnostic were really saved. Most of the time those who do something like this will make it manifestly clear that they were not saved due to their overt lack of understanding of God's grace or the fact that they are not being chastised by God at all. Hebrews 12:6-8. And I'm not trying to give a false convert false assurance for the Holy Spirit will remind one of the time they truly believed. John 14:26. And I'm not saying conclusively that all who turn their back on God seditiously and even become an atheist were never saved to begin with either.

I'm just saying that God is the One who saves and even a lapse or loss of faith doesn't mean loss of salvation. Salvation cannot be lost for any reason. And although we should remain faithful as the believer is told to walk by faith and not by sight. 1 Corinthians 4:2, 2 Corinthians 5:7, no amount of faithlessness can alter the fact that God is faithful and we are secure in His eternal hands. John 10:29.

Lamentations 3:22-23.

It is of the LORD's mercies that we are not consumed, because his compassions fail not. They are new every morning: <u>great is thy faithfulness</u>.

God bless.

3- Can Salvation Be Given Back?

It has been said that salvation can't be lost but that it can be given back or forfeited. In other words one was secure in Christ until he reaches a juncture in his or her life when the believer may renounce their faith. This idea however is unbiblical and no different from losing salvation. In the end the same outcome would come to pass in either scenario. Salvific loss and salvific forfeiture.

In discussing this issue, the confused person will inevitably say: "Now you're just talking semantics." As if the whole debate has been resolved by that silly platitude. The question is still unanswered. "Can you lose your salvation?" "Can you give your salvation back?" The answer to both is an outright:

No!

Because God who gives eternal life (John 17:2) will not take salvation back. Salvation is an indissoluble promise from God. 1 John 2:25. And it is not just any promise but a holy promise.

Psalm 105:42.

For he remembered his holy promise, and Abraham his servant.

A holy promise cannot be broken if it is to indeed be considered holy. Man is forever guilty of breaking promises but God does not. So even if a rebellious Christian turns their back, renounces his faith and gives his salvation back so to speak God's promise cannot be broken. In other words when man tries to give his salvation back or cease to be saved it cannot be done. Salvation was never about man or based on man's promise to God but has always been and always will be of God alone. (Jonah 2:9. John 1:12-14.) When a sinner gets saved it is not them promising to do anything for God but quite contrariwise them believing in what God has promised in His word to do for them. That by the death of Jesus Christ they would have eternal life through His name. (1 John 5:13. John 20:31.)

I've heard people say that there isn't one verse in the whole Bible that says that man couldn't give his salvation back. But that was an assertion grounded by ignorance because I can think of two verses right off the bat.

James 1:17.

Every good gift and every perfect gift is from above, and cometh down from the Father of lights, with whom is no variableness, neither shadow of turning.

Salvation would be included in this promise as a good and perfect gift. Romans 6:23. The fact that God's gift have no variableness or shadow of turning means He cannot take them back. And if He did take them back they would cease to be good, perfect and eternal gifts.

Look at this verse.

Romans 11:29.

For the gifts and calling of God are without repentance.

God's calling is by grace. Galatians 1:15. God's gifts are by grace as well. Ephesians 2:8-9. And according to this verse his calling and gifts are without repentance. Repentance means to change your mind and this is something God can't do when it comes to salvation. So the idea of giving salvation back is simply manmade nonsense and totally unbiblical.

God bless.

4 - OSAS And Eternal Life.

Deuteronomy 33:27.
The <u>eternal God</u> is thy refuge, and underneath are the <u>everlasting arms</u>: and he shall thrust out the enemy from before thee; and shall say, Destroy them.

Eternal security is proven simply by the words "eternal" and "everlasting" as well the cognate term: "forever." These words alone defend this wonderful doctrine because something that is eternal or everlasting literally lasts forever and cannot for any reason be terminated. When someone objects to eternal security it means that they don't have a clue what "eternal" or "everlasting" means. The Bible contains these words in both the Old Testament and the New.

But let's see how many verses there are in the New Testament where the Bible uses either of these words.

Matthew 18:8, 19:16, 19:29, 25:41, 25:46.
Mark 3:29, 10:30, 10:17.
Luke 10:25, 16:9, 18:18, 18:30.
John 3:15, 3:16, 3:36, 4:14, 4:36, 5:24, 5:39, 6:27, 6:40, 6:54, 6:68, 12:25, 17:2, 17:3.
Acts 13:46, 13:48.
Romans 1:20, 2:7, 5:31, 6:22, 6:23, 16:26.
1 Corinthians…
2 Corinthians 4:17, 4:18, 5:1.

Galatians 6:8.
Ephesians 3:11.
Philippians…
Colossians…
1 Timothy 1:16, 1:17, 6:12, 6:16, 6:19.
2 Timothy 2:10.
1 Thessalonians…
2 Thessalonians 1:9, 2:16.
Titus 1:2, 3:7.
Hebrews 5:9, 6:2, 9:12, 9:14, 9:15. 13:20.
1 Peter 5:10.
2 Peter 1:11.
1 John 1:2, 2:25, 3:15, 5:11, 5:13, 5:20.
2 John…
3 John…
Jude 1:6, 1:7, 1:21.
Revelation 14:6.

Let's look at a few of these verses.
John 17:3.
And this is life eternal, that they might know thee the only true God, and Jesus Christ, whom thou hast sent.
John 3:15.
That whosoever believeth in him should not perish, but have eternal life.
Hebrews 9:12.
Neither by the blood of goats and calves, but by his own blood he entered in once into the holy place, having obtained eternal redemption for us.
Now let's look at a few verses that refer to our salvation as being forever, hence using such rhetoric.

Isaiah 50:6.

*Lift up your eyes to the heavens, and look upon the earth beneath: for the heavens shall vanish away like smoke, and the earth shall wax old like a garment, and they that dwell therein shall die in like manner: but **my salvation shall be for ever,** and my righteousness shall not be abolished.*

Ecclesiastes 3:14.

*I know that, whatsoever God doeth, **it shall be for ever:** nothing can be put to it, nor any thing taken from it: and God doeth it, that men should fear before him.*

John 6:58.

*This is that bread which came down from heaven: not as your fathers did eat manna, and are dead: he that eateth of this bread **shall live for ever.***

Deuteronomy. 32:40.

*For I lift up my hand to heaven, and say, **I live for ever.***

2 Samuel 7:13.

*He shall build an house for my name, and I will stablish the throne of **his kingdom for ever.***

The common thread that runs throughout the Bible is the theme of eternity. This excludes any concept of losing salvation because hypothetically at the moment when it is lost it would have to cease and anything eternal, everlasting or forever cannot stop and still be true to its title. This alone should be enough to refute the idea of salvific loss. When confronted with the NOSAS people one could boldly state:

"My salvation is forever I don't know about yours.

But mine is eternal."

Like the Bible clearly, distinctly and abundantly says.

Nevertheless, someone may still claim that eternal security is not true because like the words "rapture" and "trinity" the words *eternal security* or *once saved, always saved* are not in the Bible. And sadly, that is their whole argument. But is this even true? In Job we see the concept of being secure twice.

Job 11:18.-

And thou shalt be secure, because there is hope; yea, thou shalt dig about thee, and thou shalt take thy rest in safety.

Job. 12:6-

The tabernacles of robbers prosper, and they that provoke God are secure; into whose hand God bringeth abundantly.

This should refute the argument that the concept of eternal security is not rhetorically in the Bible but in case the OSAS opponents still want to argue that this doesn't mean eternal security look at verse 11:18 again and lets break it down.

"And thou shalt be secure, because there is hope." Why is the believer secure? Because there is hope? What is hope connected to? Eternal life. (Titus 1:2.)

And to say that the actual words eternal security and once saved, always saved are not in the Bible is a fatuous strawman argument based on ignorance and a deep-seated antipathy towards the truth of God's Word.

The Bible is replete with synonyms for this

concept.
  Take a look at the following…

> *Eternal life*—John 3:15.
> *Everlasting life*—John 3:16.
> *Life eternal*—John 17:3.
> *Eternal salvation*—Hebrews 5:9.
> *Live forever*—Deuteronomy 32:40.
> *Eternal redemption*—Hebrews 9:12.
> *Everlasting covenant*—Psalm 105:10.

  Conclusion: the concept of eternal life is found all over the Bible and this incontestably proves eternal security and if one can still argue against this they are either spiritually blind, lost or just don't know what "eternal" or "everlasting" mean. Plain and simple.
  God bless.

5 - OSAS Taught By Jesus.

The greatest authority we have in the Bible is Jesus Christ. He was completely without sin. (Hebrew 4:15. 1 Peter 2:22.) So therefore what He says is veracious and He has much to say about eternal security. And this is important because God has given Jesus authority in everything that He said and done. (Matthew 7:29.)

Let's start off with His words to Martha, sister of Lazarus in John's gospel.

John 11:25-26.

Jesus said unto her, I am the resurrection, and the life: he that believeth in me, though he were dead, yet shall he live: And whosoever liveth and believeth in me **shall never die.** *Believest thou this?*

Notice carefully that Jesus is not asking Martha if she believed in Him. But rather He is asking her if she believed in OSAS or eternal security. He asked her if she believed she would never die as a result of living and simply believing in Him. Her answer was an affirmative: Yes! She believed in eternal security and knew this to be true of herself anyone else who believed in Jesus. (John 3:15-16, 3:36. 5:24, 6:47. 20:31.)

In order for one to know they are saved they must believe in the Biblical Christ. (1 John 5:20) and must believe in what He clearly promises, namely: the free gift of everlasting life to the one who simply believes in Him for it. This is how we know who the real Jesus is. The *jesus* of the NOSAS believers is not the real Jesus. He is not the way, the truth or the life as the Bible unmistakably says.

John 14:6.

Jesus saith unto him, I am the way, the truth, and the life: no man cometh unto the Father, but by me. Jesus is the truth. If we have truth we have Jesus.

Now look at the promise of:

1 John 5:12.

He that hath the Son hath life; and he that hath not the Son of God hath not life.

Having Jesus means we have Him now and forevermore.

Why? Because He lives forever. Job makes this very clear.

Job 19:25.

For I know that my redeemer liveth, and that he shall stand at the latter day upon the earth.

2 John 1:2.

For the truth's sake, which dwelleth in us, and **shall be with us for ever.**

Jesus is the truth, (John 14:6) and He will abide with the believer forever hence the believer is eternally secure.

John 14:1-3.

Let not your heart be troubled: ye believe in God, believe also in me. In my Father's house are many mansions: if it were not so, I would have told you. I go to prepare a place for you. And if I go and *prepare a place for you, I will come again, and receive you unto myself; that **where I am, there ye may be also.***

The reason why Jesus is preparing a home for us in heaven and the reason why He promises to be with us when we get there is because our salvation is secure and can't be interrupted. Not by sin, not by lack of faith. Nothing!

John 14:20.

***At that day** ye shall know that I am in my Father, and ye in me, and I in you.*

The words "at that day" denote a future state and if something could cause salvation to be lost this promise of revealing our triune unity with the Father and the Son would be invalid. But that would render God a liar and we know that cannot be. (Titus 1:2. Romans 3:3-4.)

John 17:21-24.

*That they all may be one; as thou, Father, art in me, and I in thee, that they also may be one in us: that the world may believe that thou hast sent me. And the glory which thou gavest me I have given them; that they may be one, even as we are one: I in them, and thou in me, that they may be made perfect in one; and that the world may know that thou hast sent me, and hast loved them, as thou hast loved me. Father, **I will that they also, whom thou hast given me, be with me where I am;** that they may behold my glory, which thou hast given me: for thou lovedst me before the foundation of the world.*

This also proves that we will forever be with Christ where He is in heavenly glory.

His love for us further corroborates this as well. John 13:1.

*Now before the feast of the Passover, when Jesus knew that his hour was come that he should depart out of this world unto the Father, having loved his own which were in the world, he **loved them unto the end**.*

How long does Jesus love us? Until the end. That reminds me of this verse…

Hebrews 13:5.

Let your conversation be without covetousness; and be content with such things as ye have: for he hath said, I will never leave thee, nor forsake thee.

So clearly Jesus taught eternal security and for one to not embrace this fact they are arrantly calling Him a liar.

When Jesus said: Whoever liveth and believeth in me shall never die. Believest thou this? The Once saved, always saved proponents will have no problem saying like Martha: Yea, Lord… I believe that thou art the Christ, the Son of God, which should come into the world.

The opponents however of OSAS will have to say: no … I don't. I think that my salvation can be lost and that I may end up in hell someday.

I will deal more on this subject in the next subset. God bless.

6 – And They Shall Never Perish.

Not only does the Bible teach that the believer in Christ has everlasting life, (John 6:47) it goes one step further in saying that the believer will never perish as well. This is the crux of the doctrine of eternal security.

Take a look at the following verses.

John 10:27-30.

My sheep hear my voice, and I know them, and they follow me: And I give unto them eternal life; and they shall never perish, neither shall any man pluck them out of my hand. My Father, which gave them me, is greater than all; and no man is able to pluck them out of my Father's hand. I and my Father are one.

The objectors to this verse say things like the security is conditional and only given to those who are actively following Christ and what they mean is like lemmings following a leader lemming or mice loyally following the Pied Piper. But this is not true. *Follow* in verse 27 means to <u>believe on</u>, not to literally follow like a sequacious servant adhering to his stiff-necked master's every whim and beckoning.

Zane Hodges elucidates on this verse.

"The verses in question have five clauses joined by the word *and*. A definite progression is evident. The sequence of the clauses shows that "following Him" is the condition—not the consequence—of eternal life. Jesus did not say, "I give them eternal life and they follow Me." Instead He said, "They follow Me and I give them eternal life." Since faith in Christ is the sole condition of salvation in Scripture and in John's Gospel, "following Him" must be a figure for faith in Christ."

The one who believes on Jesus has eternal life and shall never perish is the correct understanding of these verses.

John 6:37-40.

All that the Father giveth me shall come to me; and him that cometh to me I will in no wise cast out. For I came down from heaven, not to do mine own will, but the will of him that sent me. And this is the Father's will which hath sent me, that of all which he hath given me I should lose nothing, but should raise it up again at the last day. And this is the will of him that sent me, that every one which seeth the Son, and believeth on him, may have everlasting life: and I will raise him up at the last day.

These eternal security verses tell us three things. The one who comes to Christ by faith alone will never be cast out. God will lose none of His sheep and furthermore Jesus will raise the believer up at the last day.

That's: Once saved, always saved.

John 8:51-52.

Verily, verily, I say unto you, If a man keep my

saying, he shall never see death. Then said the Jews unto him, Now we know that thou hast a devil. Abraham is dead, and the prophets; and thou sayest, If a man keep my saying, he shall never taste of death.

"Keep my saying" is synonymous to "believe the gospel." And anyone who believes will never see death or taste death, translation they will never go to hell and never perish. A believer in Christ couldn't go to hell even if they wanted to. That is how eternally secure they are in Christ.

John 3:15.

That whosoever believeth in him should not perish, but have eternal life.

Clear and simple: the believer will not perish and at the same time of belief they get the permanent and irreversible free gift of eternal life. (Romans 6:23. John 4:10, Romans 5:15.)

John 11:26.

And whosoever liveth and believeth in me shall never die. Believest thou this?

Once again, the reason why the believer in Christ will never die is because they become part of the very resurrection and life of Christ, (verse 25). This promises them they will never perish!

Hebrews 2:14.

Forasmuch then as the children are partakers of flesh and blood, he also himself likewise took part of the same; that through death he might destroy him that had the power of death, that is, the devil.

Another reason why the believer in Christ will never perish is because hell is the second death, (Revelation 20:13-14) and Christ when He died on the cross for our sins, was buried and rose again triumphant—totally destroying the satanic power of death.

Revelation 20:6.

Blessed and holy is he that hath part in the first resurrection: on such the second death hath no power, but they shall be priests of God and of Christ, and shall reign with him a thousand years.

Believers in Christ have partaken of the first resurrection and therefore the second death (hell) has absolutely no power over them because they will NEVER go there. That is what they have been saved from. (John 3:17. Romans 8:1. Matthew 16:18-19.)

2 Timothy 1:10.

But is now made manifest by the appearing of our Saviour Jesus Christ, who hath abolished death, and hath brought life and immortality to light through the gospel.

The gospel means that Jesus Christ has brought eternal life to the believer as well as abolishing eternal death. Paul describes this *as so great a death* and Christ has totally delivered us from it at Calvary.

2 Corinthians 1:10.

Who delivered us from so great a death, and doth deliver: in whom we trust that he will yet deliver us.

John 6:50.

*This is the bread which cometh down from heaven, that a man may eat thereof, and **not die**.*

Revelation 2:11.

He that hath an ear, let him hear what the Spirit

saith unto the churches; He that overcometh **_shall not be hurt of the second death._**

The overcomer referred to here is the one who has believed on Jesus Christ as the Son of God. (1 John 5:4-5.) They will never be hurt of the second death.

Luke 20:36.

Neither can they die any more: for they are equal unto the angels; and are the children of God, being the <u>children of the resurrection</u>.

Only those that are unsaved will die again, born again believers can die no more. This is another clear proof for eternal security. Jesus said you must be born again. John 3:3-7, 1 John 5:1.

You must be born again, not born again and again and again because of salvific loss and recurrent faith in Christ followed by recurrent regeneration. Just like the Bible teaches: Once saved, always saved. John 11:26. It also teaches <u>once faith</u> always saved. John 6:35.

The believer is not condemned which proves that we will never perish. NEVER!

John 3:18.

He that believeth on him is not condemned: but he that believeth not is condemned already, because he hath not believed in the name of the only begotten Son of God.

Even the most famous and popular verse in the Bible affirms OSAS and that the one who simply believes on Jesus the Son of God has everlasting life and will never perish!

John 3:16.

For God so loved the world, that he gave his only

begotten Son, that whosoever believeth in him **_should not perish_**, *but have everlasting life.*

Eternal security is reinforced by the double negatives in God's Word. They are used to highlight or underscore the impossibility of the stated action occurring. In the New Testament the combination of the double negative occurs 96 times. With the light that the papyri have thrown upon this doubling of the negatives we can now say admittedly that the negatives were doubled for the sole purpose of stating denials or prohibitions emphatically—writers used the double negatives for making categorical and emphatic denials.

A double-negative is used in John 10:28. Thus John 10:28 would literally read: "they shall never (double negative) perish forever" or "Forever, they will never perish." This would sound like bad English, being somewhat redundant; but it is very strong and meaningful in the KOINE Greek in which the New Testament was written. It shows that there is no possibility of the believer ever perishing.

Hebrews 13:5.

Let your conversation be without covetousness; and be content with such things as ye have: for he hath said, I will never (ou me - never, absolutely never) *leave thee, nor* (oud ou me - never, never, absolutely never) *forsake thee.*

God bless.

7-Sealed And Secure.

One of the most important aspects of eternal security is the fact that the believer in Christ is sealed permanently by the Holy Spirit. Let's look at what the Bible says about this and see how in each verse eternal security is taught.

Romans 4:11.

And he received the sign of circumcision, a seal of the righteousness of the faith which he had yet being uncircumcised: that he might be the father of all them that believe, though they be not circumcised; that righteousness might be imputed unto them also.

By faith alone in Christ alone we get the seal of righteousness which is a permanent seal considering that it is based on God's perfect imputed righteousness and not our works. In fact God is the one who does the sealing.

John 6:27.

Labour not for the meat which perisheth, but for that meat which endureth unto everlasting life, which the Son of man shall give unto you: for him <u>hath God the Father sealed.</u>

If God seals something you can rest assured that it cannot be broken and is a permanent seal.

2 Timothy 2:19.

Nevertheless the foundation of God standeth sure, having this seal, The Lord knoweth them that are his. And, Let every one that nameth the name of Christ depart from iniquity.

This verse reveals that the seal identifies us to God and is on a sure standing foundation of God.

2 Corinthians 1:22.

Who hath also sealed us, and given the earnest of the Spirit in our hearts.

In verse 21 it says that God establishes us and anoints us as well as sealing us with the Holy Spirit. The reason why this is such a crucial subject when understanding eternal security is because the sealing is likened to a farmer branding his cattle. It is an indelible trademarking system of personal identity. We belong to God as children of God and the sealing of the Holy Spirit is like a receipt of a purchased possession. 1 Corinthians 7:23.

Ephesians 1:11-13.

In whom also we have obtained an inheritance, being predestinated according to the purpose of him who worketh all things after the counsel of his own will: That we should be to the praise of his glory, who first trusted in Christ. In whom ye also trusted, after that ye heard the word of truth, the gospel of your salvation: in whom also after that ye believed, ye were sealed with that Holy Spirit of promise.

These verses let us know that the sealing takes place instantaneous at the moment one believes the gospel and in verse 14 it is clear that the seal will remain until the praise of His glory. That means we are sealed until we get to heaven. John 12:28.

Ephesians 4:30.

And grieve not the holy Spirit of God, whereby

ye are sealed unto the day of redemption.

Now some opponents of eternal security like to say that the sealing here is no different than the sealing in Revelation 6:1 and that it can be broken due to sin. But this is impossible. Look at some examples as to why.

Daniel 12:9.

And he said, Go thy way, Daniel: for the words are closed up and sealed till the time of the end.

SEALED to the end. This excludes the idea of anything in this lifetime breaking or undoing the seal.

Ester 8:8.

Write ye also for the Jews, as it liketh you, in the king's name, and seal it with the king's ring: for the writing which is written in the king's name, and sealed with the king's ring, may no man reverse.

Like salvation, no man can reverse the seal once it is applied. Jesus' death on the cross paid it all. We can do nothing to add to this or pay for our own salvation. We can also do nothing to break or reverse this wonderful seal. Once sealed, always sealed. Once saved, always saved.

God bless.

8 - Assurance Of Salvation.

Isaiah 32:17.
And the work of righteousness shall be peace; and the effect of righteousness quietness and assurance for ever.

Hebrews 6:11.
And we desire that every one of you do show the same diligence to the full assurance of hope to the end.

Assurance of salvation and eternal security are closely related but are not necessarily the same thing. A person may be eternally secure and not have full assurance or even any assurance for that matter. Eternal security never changes and is objective. Assurance of salvation may waver depending on how deceived some may become due to demonic attacks, false doctrine or lack of sound biblical understanding on the subject.

One is eternally saved and secure the moment they believe on Christ for eternal life. John 6:35. John 10:28. But assurance is something that the believer may lose at times. One of the reasons why assurance may lack is because it is predicated on the wrong basis. One may look to his works or lifestyle and may get assurance while he is doing well, and surely that will change as he stumbles and fails.

Sadly, there are many books and sermons at large that give a false sense of assurance. The only way to have real assurance is to take God at His word. As long as you are doing that assurance will always be 100 percent. To not agree with this is to either not take God at His word or dismiss the idea that taking Him at His word is enough to give true assurance. To start out let's look at some verses where the characters in the Bible expressed assurance.

John 6:69.

And we believe and are sure that thou art that Christ, the Son of the living God.

The reason why assurance is so important is because one cannot walk the Christian walk without it. How could you walk by faith in your prayer life without assurance that you are guaranteed heaven when you die? How can you preach a sermon to hundreds of parishioners if you are not certain of your own eternal destiny? And what about evangelism? How can you tell someone else how to be saved if you aren't sure if you yourself are even saved? Assurance of salvation is of the essence of the Christian faith.

Romans 4:16.

Therefore it is of faith, that it might be by grace; to the end the promise might be sure to all the seed; not to that only which is of the law, but to that also which is of the faith of Abraham; who is the father of us all.

If one knows they are saved by grace alone

through faith alone in Christ alone then they have taken God at His word and can be sure of His eternal promise of life unending. Our assurance needs to be based on what Christ has done for us—and nothing else!

Acts 17:31.

Because he hath appointed a day, in the which he will judge the world in righteousness by that man whom he hath ordained; whereof <u>he hath given assurance</u> unto all men, in that he hath raised him from the dead.

According to this verse, God is the one who gives the assurance and it is based solely on the fact that He has already raised Jesus Christ from the dead. When a person believes on Christ, that He died, was buried and rose again; the basis of their assurance is on the fact that Christ, through God's infinite power, arose again and is in heaven awaiting them in glory. (Romans 8:34.)

1 John 5:13.

These things have I written unto you that believe on the name of the Son of God; that ye may know that ye have eternal life, and that ye may believe on the name of the Son of God.

Not only should we know we have eternal life because God said the believers in Christ do, but we should know why we have it. Look at verse 11.

1 John 5:11.

And this is the record, that God hath given to us eternal life, and this life is in his Son.

We know we have eternal life because God has already given it to us at the moment we believed in Jesus. If God gave it to us nothing can change the fact that we have it and always will. If God is powerful enough to divinely create the heavens and the earth (Genesis 1:1-7) and is powerful enough to raise Christ from the dead, (1 Corinthians 6:14) then He is powerful enough to give us eternal life. Our assurance should be based on the fact that God did what He said He did. He gave us eternal life and wants us knowing we have it. If someone doesn't have assurance of salvation it is because they haven't taken God at His word.

Plain and simple.

2 Samuel 23:5.

*Although my house be not so with God; yet he hath made with me an everlasting covenant, ordered in all things, and **sure**: for this is all my salvation, and all my desire, although he make it not to grow.*

2 Timothy 1:12.

*For the which cause I also suffer these things: nevertheless I am not ashamed: for I **know** whom I have believed, and am persuaded that he is able to keep that which I have committed unto him against that day.*

Conclusion: Assurance is not hoping *I'm saved* or being pretty sure *I'm going to heaven*. It is being 100% convinced beyond a shadow of a doubt based on the infallible promises of God word. (1 John 2:25, 2 Timothy 1:1, Titus 1:2.)

That the one who simply believes in Jesus Christ has eternal life. (John 3:15.) PERIOD!

God bless.

9 - False Eternal Security.

Since eternal security is so integral we must know and beware that there is a false version of it. There are many people out there teaching a type of security that isn't biblical and isn't eternal security at all. (Conditional security) in other words ... a believer is secure as long as he remains close to Christ, doesn't sin as much and perseveres to the end. But this isn't security at all.

The Bible makes it clear that if one obeys the whole law and then fails in one point he is guilty of all. James 2:10. This type of security gives no realistic sinner any real comfort, assurance or hope. And why would it? If one had to live a certain way to be secure then why would they need security at all. Just live right and everything will be okay. But the Bible teaches unconditional eternal security.

Titus 3:5.

Not by works of righteousness which we have done, but according to his mercy he saved us, by the washing of regeneration, and renewing of the Holy Ghost.

False eternal security, contrary to what most teach, is not that of the one who lives like the devil and thinks he will still go to heaven. False security is thinking that you can't live like the devil and still be secure. In reality, eternal security means that you can live anyway you want to and still go to heaven. Nevertheless God still desires that we serve Him as a result of our eternal security. (Hebrews 12:28, 2 Corinthians 5:15, Titus 2:11-12. 2 Corinthians 7:1, John 14:15, Titus 3:8, 2 Timothy 3:17.)

Just because God desires this and the fact that the scriptures abjure obedience doesn't mean that believers will automatically obey—and whether they do or not doesn't change the fact that they are eternally secure. John 10:35.

The truth is sin doesn't pay and has awful consequences (Romans 6:23, James 1:15, Galatians 6:7-8.) However where sin abounds grace does much more abound, (Romans 5:20.) As sinners, we should recognize how sinful we are and not pretend like we are not that bad. Romans 3:9-12, 23). Moreover, that is exactly what this fake Lordship version of security does. Since it won't allow Christians to backslide, commit gross sins, fall away ... etc. it has minimized our understanding about sin and just how sinful we actually are. (Romans 7:8-20.)

The main problem with fake eternal security is that it looks to a person and how he lives (in the future) and not to the full sufficiency of Christ and the finished work of the cross. (John 19:30, Hebrews 12:2.)

Those that are saved and understand real eternal security know that their salvation has already been paid for and nothing in the future can change or effect it. (2 Timothy 1:9.) Those that think that some sin or event can prove one to not be saved have not understood the past reality of salvation. Instead of resting in God's eternal promise these people who espouse a false security look for verses to wrest out of context in order to erroneously bolster their nefarious claims. And this is really no different than the one who thinks salvation can be lost.

Arminians believe salvation can be lost. Calvinists believe you can't lose salvation but you can prove you never had it in the first place—if you fall away or don't endure to the end. Frankly, I don't see what the difference is between both damnable systems.

Free grace proponents know that they are saved and secure whether they persevere to the end or not: (1 John 5:13.) The reason why this false security is so dangerous is because it gives anyone who is honest about themselves reason to doubt their salvation.

Real eternal security can be defined as this. A sinners hears the gospel and simply believes on Jesus Christ to save them and then they live the same way they used to or even worse (perhaps even committing murder or suicide) and they still go to heaven when they die—because of the grace of God. (Romans 5:15.)

Most people will not agree with this but then again most people are on the broad path to destruction anyway. (Matthew 7:13-14.)

Eternal security is based on the character of God and His immutable promise. The most powerful verse in my opinion is John 5:24. This verse affirms real eternal security.

John 5:24.

Verily, verily, I say unto you, He that heareth my word, and believeth on him that sent me, hath everlasting life, and shall not come into condemnation; but is passed from death unto life.

Look at the tenses of salvation in this verse.

Hath everlasting life… (Present tense.)

Shall not come into condemnation… (Future tense.)

Is passed from death unto life… (Present tense.)

One cannot get any more eternally secure than this.

Conclusion. As Christians we should not for any reason think salvation can be lost. We shouldn't think that someone can't lose their salvation but prove they never had it to begin with either. But should know that the one who believes in Jesus is eternally secure no matter what and we have God's Word guaranteeing it. (John 6:39-40.)

False security comes from a manmade system of theology. Calvinism and Lordship salvation are responsible for this false security. Calvinism is so evil I made a list of reasons why anyone who has always believed in 5-point TULIP theology is lost and until they repent of it and believe the real gospel of free grace theology they are doomed to hell.

Here are ten reasons why…

1. Calvinists say you can't come to Christ which means they haven't come to Christ which

means Jesus is referring to them (you will not come to me that you may have life) in John 5:40 and therefore they are going to hell.
2. They say Jesus only died for the elect. The Bible says Jesus died for all. Hebrews 2:9. Their Jesus is a liar and a liar can't be the Saviour. Hebrews 4:15.
3. They believe one must persevere to the end which is works and works won't save. Galatians 2:16.
4. They believe in another Jesus who doesn't have the power to save all. So they are believing in a Jesus that can't save. 2 Corinthians 11:3-5.
5. They don't believe that anyone who believes in Jesus has everlasting life and how could they if the non-elect aren't chosen to have faith. So therefore they don't believe the Bible in John 6:47.
6. They can't have assurance if Jesus didn't die for everyone. Assurance is the essence of saving faith so they don't have real faith and are unbelievers who are condemned. John 3:18.
7. They have another name. John Calvin. Jesus Christ is the only name that saves. Acts 4:12.
8. They reject scripture and change words to mean something they don't mean. "World" to "elect," all doesn't really mean all. John 8:43-48.
9. They reject free will. Without free will there is no receiving salvation. Revelation 22:17.

And finally—10. Their father is Satan. John 8:44.

The main thing we need to understand is that there is a huge difference between fake security and real security and it really just boils down to the distinction between law and grace. Here is a chart that dichotomously separates the two.

Grace.	Law.
Salvation. Ephesians 2:8.	Damnation.
OSAS. John 10:28.	NOSAS.
Justification. Romans 3:28.	Condemnation.
Freedom. Galatians 4:7	Legalism.
Real Jesus. John 14:6.	False Jesus.
Believe only. Acts 16:31.	Repent of sins.
Done. John 19:30.	Do...

God bless.

10 - What Is Faith? (Regarding O.S.A.S)

There is much discussion about faith and many false teachers are redefining what faith is in order to deceive people (2 Corinthians 2:17, 4:2.) So let's take a look at the Bible and see how it defines faith.

Hebrews 11:1.

Now faith is the substance of things hoped for, the evidence of things not seen.

Faith is a persuasion not a decision. One does not decide to believe something is true without first being persuaded that it is true and if one is persuaded he has already believed it. Namely, that the one who believes on Jesus has what Jesus said … everlasting life. John 6:47.

Here are a list of things faith is not.
1. Obedience.
2. Surrender.
3. Commitment.
4. Repentance.
5. Sorrow for sin.
6. Good works.
7. Holiness.
8. Making Christ Lord of your life.
9. Persevering to the end.

10. Behaving.

Faith is knowing something to be true.

John 10:38.

But if I do, though ye believe not me, believe the works: that ye may <u>know, and believe</u>, that the Father is in me, and I in him.

Faith brings assurance.

Romans 8:21-22.

And being fully persuaded that, what he had promised, he was able also to perform. And therefore it was imputed to him for righteousness.

Abraham was fully persuaded and then God imputed His righteousness to his account. That means being fully persuaded was the same as having faith.

Romans 8:38.

For I am persuaded, that neither death, nor life, nor angels, nor principalities, nor powers, nor things present, nor things to come.

Conclusion:

Faith is being convinced that something is true. If one does not believe OSAS they are not convinced that the Bible is true so therefore such people don't have biblical faith. Those that believe OSAS or eternal security have believed on Christ and are fully persuaded that they have eternal life that can never be lost because that is what the Bible says. That is faith.

Jesus said that the one who believes on me has everlasting life. John 3:15, 16, 6:47. One either believes this or they do not. If they do that is faith. If not that is unbelief.

John 20:27.

Then saith he to Thomas, Reach hither thy finger, and behold my hands; and reach hither thy hand, and thrust it into my side: and be not faithless, but believing.

Here is a list of NT verses that make it clear that salvation is by faith or believing alone.

Luke 7:48-50; 8:12; 18:42 John 1:7, 12; 2:23; 3:15, 16, 18, 36; 4:39; 4:41, 42; 5:24, 45-47; 6:29, 35, 40, 47; 7:38, 39; 8:24, 29, 30; 9:35-38; 10:24-26; 11:15, 25, 26, 41, 42; 12:36, 46; 13:19; 14:1-6, 17:20, 21; 19:35; 20:29, 31. Acts 3:16; 4:4, 32; 8:12, 37; 9:42; 10:43, 45; 11:17, 21; 13:21, 39; 14:1, 23, 27; 15:7, 9; 16:31; 17:4, 5, 11, 12; 18:8, 27; 19:4; 20:21; 21:25; 26:18. Romans 1:16, 17; 3:22, 25, 26, 27, 28, 30; 4:3, 5, 9, 11, 13, 16, 23, 24; 5:1, 2; 9:30, 32, 33; 10:4, 6, 9, 10; 11:20, 30-32; 15:13. 1 Corinthians 1:21. 2 Corinthians 4:4. Galatians 2:16, 20; 3:2, 5, 6, 7, 8, 9, 11, 14, 22, 24, 26; 5:5. Ephesians 1:13, 19; 2:8; 3:17. Philippians 1:29; 3:9 1 Thessalonians 1:7; 2:10; 4:14. 2 Thessalonians 1:10; 2:12, 13; 3:2. 1 Timothy 1:16; 3:16; 4:3, 10. 2 Timothy 1:12; 3:15. Hebrews 4:2, 3; 6:12; 10:39; 11:6, 7, 31. James 2:23. 1 Peter 1:21; 2:6, 7. 1 John 5:1, 5, 10, 13. Jude 5.
  God bless.

11- Problem Passages Explained.

There are scores of passages in the Bible that heretics use to try to refute eternal security by twisting them out of context. This must be dealt with so that false prophets can be scripturally refuted and the truth of this doctrine will forever stand. (1 Peter 1:23-25.)

Let's deal with these verses in the proper context one by one.

James 2:20-21.

But wilt thou know, O vain man, that faith without works is dead? Was not Abraham our father justified by works, when he had offered Isaac his son upon the altar? Seest thou how faith wrought with his works, and by works was faith made perfect?

They try to say that one must have works in accompaniment to faith and that flatly denies salvation by faith alone. This of course would refute eternal security as well if one didn't abide in good works until the end of their life. But this doesn't work because James was not written to unbelievers and is not about evangelism at all. The gospel of John is purposed for that. (John 20:31.)

In fact, James was written to believers. (James 1:2, brethren.)

Another thing to remember is James is dealing with justification before man not before God. Justification unto salvation from God is by faith alone. (Romans 3:21-28, 5:1. Ephesians 2:8-9.) The doctrine of eternal security is not refuted by this because James is not dealing with eternal salvation at all.

Hebrews 6:4-6.

For it is impossible for those who were once enlightened, and have tasted of the heavenly gift, and were made partakers of the Holy Ghost, And have tasted the good word of God, and the powers of the world to come, If they shall fall away, to renew them again unto repentance; seeing they crucify to themselves the Son of God afresh, and put him to an open shame.

This is usually referring to believers falling away and so-called losing salvation. But this is not dealing with loss of salvation but loss of rewards. All this is saying is that Christ cannot be crucified again because He only died once. Romans 6:9-10. He can't be crucified again because He doesn't need to be. People should not be using the book of Hebrews to combat eternal security considering that there are many verses in Hebrews that clearly champion it. (Hebrews 9:12, 5:9, 7:25. 10:14.)

Hebrews 10:26-28.

For if we sin wilfully after that we have received the knowledge of the truth, there remaineth no more sacrifice for sins, But a certain fearful looking for of judgment and fiery indignation, which shall devour the adversaries. He that despised Moses' law died without mercy under two or three witnesses: Of how much sorer punishment, suppose ye, shall he be thought worthy, who hath trodden under foot the Son of God, and hath counted the blood of the covenant, wherewith he was sanctified, an unholy thing, and hath done despite unto the Spirit of grace?

The heretics try to say that if someone continues to wilfully sin they will lose their salvation. This is nonsense because all sins have been washed away by the blood of Jesus. (Past, present and future.) 1 John 1:7. The wilful sins here is referring to rejecting Christ and going back to animal sacrifices. If someone is unsaved and they reject God's free grace and go back to a works-based system there is no more sacrifice for sins and one remains lost. That is all this verse is talking about.

1 Corinthians 6:9-10.

Know ye not that the unrighteous shall not inherit the kingdom of God? Be not deceived: neither fornicators, nor idolaters, nor adulterers, nor effeminate, nor abusers of themselves with mankind, Nor thieves, nor covetous, nor drunkards, nor revilers, nor extortioners, shall inherit the kingdom of God.

The heretics use these verses to try to say that if one commits the sins on this list they will lose their salvation and go to hell. But this is not referring to the saved at all. Considering that it starts off describing the sinners here as the unrighteous. The saved have God's imputed righteousness and are never considered unrighteous positionally.

(Romans 4:11, 24-25. Philippians 3:9.) Besides they forget to read verse 11 which declares believers as: washed, sanctified and justified.

Revelation 21:8.

But the fearful, and unbelieving, and the abominable, and murderers, and whoremongers, and sorcerers, and idolaters, and all liars, shall have their part in the lake which burneth with fire and brimstone: which is the second death.

The heretics say that if you commit one of these sins you will lose salvation and go to hell. But this can't be true. Number one all sin has been forgiven and washed away by the blood of Jesus. Ephesians 4:32. Colossians 2:13, Titus 2:14. One needs to just go back to verse 7 to see that verse 8 is referring to the unsaved.

Revelation 21:7.

He that overcometh shall inherit all things; and I will be his God, and he shall be my son.

"Overcometh" just means saved by faith in Jesus Christ. 1 John 5:4-5.

All believers in Christ are overcomers and blood-bought children of God, (Galatians 3:26, 1 John 5:1, John 1:12-13, Galatians 4:6,) and all children of God go to heaven. 1 John 3:2. John 14:1-3.

The "but" in verse 8 divides children of God with the unsaved. And that is the only reason why they go to hell. Because they were unsaved unbelievers their entire life. (John 3:18, 3:36. 8:24.)

Matthew 24:23.

But he that shall endure unto the end, the same shall be saved. See also: Matthew 10:22.

The heretics claim you must endure to the end to

finally be saved and those that don't endure will lose salvation. The problem with this is one receives the free gift of eternal life instantaneously the moment they believe on Christ. (John 3:36, 5:24. 6:47.) This verse is talking about enduring to the end of the tribulation and being saved physically. I.e., (not taking the mark of the beast.) See Matthew 24:22, it is a reference to the flesh being saved. These passages have nothing to do with eternal life and salvation. Heaven or hell.

Galatians 5:4.

Christ is become of no effect unto you, whosoever of you are justified by the law; ye are fallen from grace.

The heretics try to say that "falling from grace" means salvific loss. But it does not, falling from grace means falling from the principle of grace and how does one do that? Simple. By recidivating back to a works system for justification. The ones doing this ironically are those who add works or believe that salvation can be lost. The saved can never fall from grace because it goes on into eternity. Romans 5:20-21. And comes from an eternal God. Titus 2:12, 3:7.

Conclusion. There are **NO** verses that teach salvation can be lost. If there were then God's Word would contradict itself and that can never happen. (Titus 1:2. Hebrews 6:17-18.)

God bless.

12- OSAS And Sin.

Opponents of eternal security tend to use sin to make people think they can lose their salvation. But sin is the very thing Christ came to this earth to die for. (1 Corinthians 15:1-4. John 1:29. 1 John 3:5.)

How on earth can sin keep someone from heaven if Christ died for sinners? Romans 5:6-8. The reason people believe that sin can cause them to lose their salvation is because they haven't believed that Jesus paid for anything at the cross. They literally believe that the cross accomplished nothing. Anyone who rejects eternal security has done so by not believing the Bible in many doctrinal areas. Here are many scriptural examples of characters in the Bible sinning horrible sins who were eternally secure and went to heaven.

1 Corinthians 5:1-5.

It is reported commonly that there is fornication among you, and such fornication as is not so much as named among the Gentiles, that one should have his father's wife. And ye are puffed up, and have not rather mourned, that he that hath done this deed might be taken away from among you. For I verily, as absent in body, but present in spirit, have judged already, as though I were present, concerning him that hath so done this deed, In the name of our Lord Jesus Christ, when ye are gathered together, and my spirit, with the power of our Lord Jesus Christ, To deliver such an one unto Satan for the destruction of the flesh, that the spirit may be saved in the day of the Lord Jesus.

This is about as bad as it gets in most people's eyes. Incestuous fornication and he still went to heaven. We know this by the fact that it said the spirit may be saved in the day of the Lord Jesus.

1 Corinthians 10:1-11.

Moreover, brethren, I would not that ye should be ignorant, how that all our fathers were under the cloud, and all passed through the sea; And were all baptized unto Moses in the cloud and in the sea; And did all eat the same spiritual meat; And did all drink the same spiritual drink: for they drank of that spiritual Rock that followed them: and that Rock was Christ. But with many of them God was not well pleased: for they were overthrown in the wilderness. Now these things were our examples, to the intent we should not lust after evil things, as they also lusted. Neither be ye idolaters, as were some of them; as it is written, The people sat down to eat and drink, and rose up to play. Neither let us commit fornication, as some of them committed, and fell in one day three and twenty thousand. Neither let us tempt Christ, as some of them also tempted, and were destroyed of serpents. Neither murmur ye, as some of them also murmured, and were destroyed of the destroyer. Now all these things happened unto them for examples: and they are written for our admonition, upon whom the ends of the world are come.

Paul identifies them as believers in the first few verses. Baptized unto Moses, they drank of the rock of Christ. Yet they were behaving like ungodly heathen as they fornicated, got drunk, worshipped idols and tempted Christ.

1 Corinthians 3:11-15.

For other foundation can no man lay than that is laid, which is Jesus Christ. Now if any man build upon this foundation gold, silver, precious stones, wood, hay, stubble; Every man's work shall be made manifest: for the day shall declare it, because it shall be revealed by fire; and the fire shall try every man's work of what sort it is. If any man's work abide which he hath built thereupon, he shall receive a reward. If any man's work shall be burned, he shall suffer loss: but he himself shall be saved; yet so as by fire.

This makes it clear that there will be some believers who did nothing with their lives and lived a wasteful, sinful profligate lifestyle and were still saved yet they will receive no reward.

Psalms 89:28-34.

My mercy will I keep for him for evermore, and my covenant shall stand fast with him. His seed also will I make to endure for ever, and his throne as the days of heaven. If his children forsake my law, and walk not in my judgments; If they break my statutes, and keep not my commandments; Then will I visit their transgression with the rod, and their iniquity with stripes. Nevertheless my lovingkindness will I not utterly take from him, nor suffer my faithfulness to fail. My covenant will I not break, nor alter the thing that is gone out of my lips.

Here is an example of saved people forsaking God's laws, breaking the commandments and walking not in His judgments and yet they were still saved. Why? Because God's faithfulness never fails. (Lamentations 3:22-23. 1 Corinthians 1:9. 1 Peter 4:19.)

Here is an example of a believer overtaken by a fault. Does the Bible say that they weren't really saved or that they lost their salvation? No it says that a spiritual believer should help restore him.

Galatians 6:1.

Brethren, if a man be overtaken in a fault, ye which are spiritual, restore such an one in the spirit of meekness; considering thyself, lest thou also be tempted.

An unsaved person once dared me to show him any passage of scripture that proves that a sinner engaged in active sin would still go to heaven. He rejected the clear teaching of eternal security and was trying to earn his salvation. But to take him up on his challenge let's look at Daniel 9. Look at how many times these people were referred to as sinners who were actively sinning yet the conclusion was that they were saved, forgiven and heaven-bound by the grace of God.

Daniel 9:4-9.

And I prayed unto the LORD my God, and made my confession, and said, O Lord, the great and dreadful God, keeping the covenant and mercy to them that love him, and to them that keep his commandments; <u>We have sinned</u>, and have <u>committed iniquity</u>, and <u>have done wickedly</u>, and have <u>rebelled</u>, even by <u>departing from thy precepts</u> and from thy judgments: Neither have we hearkened unto thy servants the prophets, which *spake in thy name to our kings, our princes, and our fathers, and to all the people of the land. O* LORD, *righteousness belongeth unto thee, but unto us confusion of faces, as at this day; to the men of Judah, and to the inhabitants of Jerusalem, and unto all Israel, that are near, and that are far off, through all the countries whither thou hast driven them, because of <u>their trespass that they have trespassed against thee</u>. O Lord, to us belongeth confusion of face, to our kings, to our princes, and to our fathers, because <u>we have sinned against thee</u>. To the Lord our God belong mercies and forgivenesses, though we have rebelled against him.*

Look at the last few sentences. "To the Lord our God belong mercies and forgivenesses, though we have rebelled against him." That's eternal security to a totally sinful people who deserved nothing more than the eternal torments of hellfire and damnation.

Yet they received forgiveness and mercy. Why? Because: Once saved, always saved is true. Not even the grossest of sins can alter this wonderful promise of God. (1 John 2:25. John 10:28. Romans 8:38-39.)

Jesus, after abjuring us not to sin, tells us in John's first epistle that we are inevitably going to sin and when this happens we have an advocate with the Father. How is salvific loss possible if Jesus Christ keeps defending us as we recurrently sin? It isn't.

1 John 2:1.

My little children, these things write I unto you,

that ye sin not. And if any man sin, we have an advocate with the Father, Jesus Christ the righteous.

The reason why no sin can cause a believer to go to hell is because Christ paid for all our sins in full. (John 19:30.)

Colossians 2:13.

And you, being dead in your sins and the uncircumcision of your flesh, hath he quickened together with him, having forgiven you all trespasses.

Psalm 103:12.

As far as the east is from the west, so far hath he removed our transgressions from us.

Hebrews 10:17.

And their sins and iniquities will I remember no more.

The truth is: we all sin. Galatians 3:22, Romans 3:23, 5:12. Ecclesiastes 7:20. And if once saved, always saved were not true then NO ONE (because of sin) would be going to heaven. Because: Once saved, always saved is true no believer in Christ (because of sins) can ever go to hell. We are eternally secure.

I'm not trying to downplay sin by any means. Sin has separated unbelievers from God. Isaiah 59:2. We are all guilty sinners who deserve condemnation in hell. Romans 3:9-12, 19, 23. God hates sin. Psalm 5:4, 11:5, 45:6-7. The point is all sin is covered by the payment Christ made for us. (2 Corinthians 5:21.)

And all our sins are gone!

MY SINS ARE GONE.

You ask me why I'm happy so I'll just tell you why, because my sins are gone; And when I meet the scoffers who ask me where they are, I say, "My sins are gone."

Chorus…
They're underneath the blood on the cross of Calvary, As far removed as darkness is from dawn; in the sea of God's forgetfulness, that's good enough for me, Praise God, my sins are gone!

'Twas at the old-time altar where God came in my heart and now my sins are gone; the Lord took full possession, the devil did depart, I'm glad my sins are gone!

When Satan comes to tempt me and tries to make me doubt, I say, "My sins are gone, You got me into trouble but Jesus got me out." I'm glad my sins are gone!

I'm living now for Jesus, I'm happy night and day, Because my sins are gone; my soul is filled with music, with all my heart I say, "I know my sins are gone!"

****

Here is a list of famous characters in the Bible who were all saved (Hebrews 11:1-40,) and yet committed horrible sins.

Rahab the Harlot… harlotry. Joshua 6:17.
David… fornication and murder. 2 Samuel 11:1-6.
Jacob… lying. Genesis 25:33.
Lot… incest, drunkenness. Genesis 19:32-34.
Paul… carnality. Romans 7.
Peter… denying Christ. Mark 14:30.
Moses… murder. Exodus 2:12.
Samson… fornication. Judges 16:1.
Noah… drunkenness. Genesis 9:21.
The church of Corinth. 1 Corinthians 10:1-12.
Jonah … running from God. Jonah 1:3.
You and I (everyone.) Romans 3:23.
   God bless.

13- OSAS And The Gospel.

For **G**od so loved the world, that he gave his
    Only begotten
    Son, that whosoever believeth in him should not
    Perish, but have
    Everlasting
    Life……………. John 3:16.

The gospel message is the Good News of salvation by grace through faith alone.

Acts 13:32-33.

And we declare unto you <u>glad tidings</u>, how that the promise which was made unto the fathers, God hath fulfilled the same unto us their children, in that he hath raised up Jesus again; as it is also written in the second psalm, Thou art my Son, this day have I begotten thee.

Luke 2:10.

And the angel said unto them, Fear not: for, behold, I bring you <u>good tidings</u> of great joy, which shall be to all people.

The word "tidings" which means message is found all over the Bible. 2 Samuel 4:4, 4:10, 13:30. Isaiah 61:1. But in the gospel of Luke it is not just some ordinary message but a good message. Literally: Good News. That is exactly what the gospel is.

The greatest news in the world!

Eternal security is good news and therefore crucial if one is preaching the true gospel of grace.

We are told to preach the gospel to everyone. Mark 16:15.

And he said unto them, Go ye into all the world, and preach the gospel to every creature.

But once again, can someone honestly preach the true gospel without expounding eternal security? No.

The true gospel must be one of eternal grace. Romans 5:20-21.

Galatians 1:4-5.

Who gave himself for our sins, that he might deliver us from this present evil world, according to the will of God and our Father: To whom be glory for ever and ever. Amen. I marvel that ye are so soon removed from him that called you into the grace of Christ unto another gospel.

Any other gospel is another gospel.

Galatians 1:8-9.

But though we, or an angel from heaven, preach any other gospel unto you than that which we have preached unto you, let him be accursed. As we said before, so say I now again, if any man preach any other gospel unto you than that ye have received, let him be accursed.

Losing salvation is another gospel just like a works based salvation, Calvinism and Lordship salvation. The true gospel is grace alone through faith alone in Christ alone and the believer is eternally secure.

Now what does it mean to believe the gospel. The gospel is the death, burial and resurrection of our Lord and Saviour Jesus Christ.

1 Corinthians 15:3-4.

For I delivered unto you first of all that which I also received, how that Christ died for our sins according to the scriptures; And that he was buried, and that he rose again the third day according to the scriptures.

Here are some other passages that convey the same message: 1 Thessalonians 4:14. Luke 24:7. John 2:19-20.

The gospel is the message of how one is saved. When one believes on Jesus Christ He should know that Jesus dying on the cross for him is why he is eternally saved. We recognize that we deserve to go to hell and be punished forever.

However because Jesus died on the cross for us the believer will never go to hell. It is what He did for us that won't allow us to be condemned: John 3:18, 5:24, Romans 8:1.

Luke 24:20.

And how the chief priests and our rulers delivered him to be condemned to death, and have crucified him.

Christ took our condemnation for us. (Romans 8:3.)

We can't be condemned because He was condemned in our place. 1 Peter 3:18.
If one thinks he can still end up in hell for whatever reason, he has not really believed the gospel message and is not trusting in Jesus Christ or what He did for him/her at all.

The Bible says:

Romans 5:8.

But God commendeth his love toward us, in that, while we were yet sinners, Christ died for us.

Because Jesus Christ died for everyone those who trust Him alone are forever saved. To believe the gospel is to know with 100 percent certainty that you will never go to hell and are going to heaven ... because and only because of what Christ did for you at the cross of Calvary.

This is the crux of eternal security. We are secure because of the gospel.

Romans 1:16.

For I am not ashamed of the gospel of Christ: for it is the power of God unto salvation to every one that believeth; to the Jew first, and also to the Greek.

Jesus didn't die so we could have temporary life; no He died to freely give us eternal life. (John 17:2-3. John 10:28. 1 John 5:11.)

Conclusion.

You cannot preach the gospel message divorced from the doctrine of eternal security. In fact any other message is counterfactual to the gospel. Eternal security and the gospel are one and the same. Evangelism is incomplete without it.

The eternal Saviour died so that we through faith in Him will eternally live.

Galatians 2:20.

I am crucified with Christ: nevertheless I live; yet not I, but Christ liveth in me: and the life which I now live in the flesh I live by the faith of the Son of God, who loved me, and gave himself for me.

God bless.

14 - Objections To OSAS.

To all the many objections of eternal security there is usually an underlying reason. Below is a list of reasons why people do not believe in: Once saved, always saved.

1—Lost.
2 Corinthians 4:3-4.
But if our gospel be hid, it is hid to them that are lost: In whom the god of this world hath blinded the minds of them which believe not, lest the light of the glorious gospel of Christ, who is the image of God, should shine unto them.

Plain and simple. They are lost and have been blinded to the truth of eternal security.

Ephesians 2:12.
That at that time ye were without Christ, being aliens from the commonwealth of Israel, and strangers from the covenants of promise, having no hope, and without God in the world.

The fact that they don't know God is why they don't believe the truth of eternal security. God has not revealed it to them like He has to the believer in Christ. John 14:26.

2—Unbelief.
John 3:18.

He that believeth on him is not condemned: but he that believeth not is condemned already, because he hath not believed in the name of the only begotten Son of God.

John 3:36.

He that believeth on the Son hath everlasting life: and he that believeth not the Son shall not see life; but the wrath of God abideth on him.

1 John 5:10.

He that believeth on the Son of God hath the witness in himself: he that believeth not God hath made him a liar; because <u>he believeth not the record that God gave of his Son.</u>

They do not believe what the Bible teaches and that is why they do not believe in eternal security.

3—Carnality.

1 Corinthians 3:1-3.

And I, brethren, could not speak unto you as unto spiritual, but as unto carnal, even as unto babes in Christ. I have fed you with milk, and not with meat: for hitherto ye were not able to bear it, neither yet now are ye able. For ye are yet carnal: for whereas there is among you envying, and strife, and divisions, are ye not carnal, and walk as men?

Their carnality keeps them blind from spiritual truths. 1 Corinthians 2:12-16.

4—Wrong teaching. False prophets.

Matthew 7:15.

Beware of false prophets, which come to you in sheep's clothing, but inwardly they are ravening wolves.

They have been listening to the wrong teachers for too long and can't discern what the truth is.

(Hebrews 5:14.)

5—Ignorance.

Matthew 22:29.

Jesus answered and said unto them, Ye do err, not knowing the scriptures, nor the power of God.

Ignorance of God's word is also ignorance to the power of God as found in His word. Denial of eternal security means you deny that God has the power to raise sinful believers from their deadness. If one weren't ignorant to God's word and would actually believe it they wouldn't be ignorant of His power and would know that it is the power of God that makes eternal security true. 1 Peter 1:4-5.

Ephesians 4:18.

Having the understanding darkened, being alienated from the life of God through the ignorance that is in them, because of the blindness of their heart.

6—Hate for the truth.

2 Thessalonians 2:10.

And with all deceivableness of unrighteousness in them that perish; because they received not the love of the truth, that they might be saved.

In many cases people just hate the truth of scripture and that is why they reject the Bible's most central truth of eternal security.

7—Reprobation.

2 Timothy 3:7.

Ever learning, and never able to come to the knowledge of the truth.

They are reprobates and have rejected the truth over and over again insofar that God as given them over to a reprobate mind and therefore they cannot come to the truth. See also: John 12:39-40.

8—Twisting verses out of context.

2 Peter 3:16.

As also in all his epistles, speaking in them of these things; in which are some things hard to be understood, which they that are unlearned and unstable wrest, as they do also the other scriptures, unto their own destruction.

Many of the rejecters of eternal security have done so because they have twisted verses out of context. That is the only way to get to a false teaching because no clear passages teach anything false. (John 3:16, Acts 16:31. Ephesians 2:8-9.)

9—They haven't fully trusted Christ.

Psalm 78:22.

Because they believed not in God, and trusted not in his salvation.

The main reason people do not believe in eternal security is because they are not or have not fully trusted Christ for their salvation. They still think it is up to them not to mess up in the future for fear that they might lose it. Ultimately salvation is up to them. Those that believe in once saved, always saved have fully trusted in Christ and know that they are saved, have eternal life and are eternally secure and it is all based on what Christ has already done for us when He died for our sins at the cross of Calvary 2000 years ago. (John 19:30.)

Thank God eternal security is true because if it weren't no one would be going to heaven!

Conclusion: Whatever reason these heretics have for denying the clear teaching of eternal security it is always because of rejecting the Word of God and never a result of taking it as veridical truth thus allowing it to set the believer free. John 8:32-33.

God bless.

15 - Faith Is Not A Work.

The Calvinists will say that if you don't believe all their TULIP garbage then you having faith in Christ is a work or a form of human merit. Unless God regenerates us first, they deem, and gives us faith as a gift then it must be a work.
Why do they say this?
For two reasons.
To try to discredit others faith and to prove that they don't believe that anyone who simply believes on Jesus has everlasting life, which would in turn evoke that they are still lost.
They say that the only way faith is not a work is if God gives it to us as a gift. But is this true? Absolutely not. Faith is not a gift; salvation is the gift. Romans 6:23. Faith comes by hearing and hearing by the word of God. Romans 10:17.
It doesn't come by regeneration. The truth is faith has no merit. Only Jesus Christ and the finished work of the cross have saving merit. Here are some basic reasons why faith is not a work by any means.

1—God tells us in His word that salvation is not of works. Ephesians 2:8-9. 2 Timothy 1:9. But then tells us to believe on Christ. (Acts 16:31. 1 John 3:23.) God would never tell us to believe or have faith if it were a work.

2—Faith is not what technically (semantically) saves; it is grace that saves through faith. Ephesians 2:8-9.

3—Faith is accompanied by "working not." Romans 4:5.

But to him that worketh not, but believeth on him that justifieth the ungodly, his faith is counted for righteousness.

4—Anyone can have faith.
John 1:7.

The same came for a witness, to bear witness of the Light, that all men through him might believe.

Sure the Holy Spirit must draw us and the gospel must be preached and lucidly heard. John 6:44. John 16:8-11. Romans 10:17, Romans 1:16. But this applies to everyone. Anyone can hear the gospel and respond to it in faith. If it were only for certain people then it would be meritorious but since anyone can have faith it has no merit. God has enabled everyone to have faith. Romans 12:3.

5—it's not our faith but the faith of Christ.
Romans 3:22.

Even the righteousness of God which is by <u>faith of Jesus Christ</u> unto all and upon all them that believe: for there is no difference.

See also Galatians 3:22.

6—Faith comes from grace.
Acts 18:27.

And when he was disposed to pass into Achaia, the brethren wrote, exhorting the disciples to receive him: who, when he was come, helped them much which had <u>believed through grace</u>.

Grace and works are incompatible and

immiscible. (Romans 11:6.)

7—Faith is merely a channel and Christ is the sole object of our faith.

1 Timothy 1:14.

And the grace of our Lord was exceeding abundant with faith and love which is in Christ Jesus.

1 Timothy 3:13.

For they that have used the office of a deacon well purchase to themselves a good degree, and great boldness in the faith which is in Christ Jesus.

2 Timothy 1:13.

Hold fast the form of sound words, which thou hast heard of me, in faith and love which is in Christ Jesus.

2 Timothy 3:15.

And that from a child thou hast known the holy scriptures, which are able to make thee wise unto salvation through faith which is in Christ Jesus.

He is the one who completely saves.

John 3:17.

For God sent not his Son into the world to condemn the world; but that the world through him might be saved.

Conclusion.

Jesus Christ said in many places that the one who simply believes on Him has everlasting life (John 3:36, 6:47, and 6:40.) Belief is never a work. One either believes or they don't. I believe.

God bless.

16 - OSAS And Greek Tenses.

Acts 19:4.
Then said Paul, John verily baptized with the baptism of repentance, saying unto the people, that they should <u>believe</u> on him which should come after him, that is, on Christ Jesus.

The Bible makes it clear that one must believe on Jesus Christ to be saved; but must one continue to believe or is a moment of belief all that is necessary to have everlasting life?

John 3:16.
For God so loved the world, that he gave his only begotten Son, that whosoever believeth in him should not perish, but have everlasting life.

John 3:16 doesn't say: "whosoever continues to believe" but some will misuse the Greek tense to make naive people think that they must continue to believe in order to be saved. But after actually studying the Greek nothing could be further from the truth. In reality, the Greek tenses help us understand that it is a moment of belief and not continual belief like the heretics and deniers of eternal security posit.

The phrase "whosever believeth" in John 3:16 is not a simple present tense as some contend in order to demand that one must maintain a constant state of believing so that one will continue to possess eternal life otherwise lose it; rather, as previously indicated, it is the relative pronoun "whosoever" with the definite article "ho" = "the" and the present, active nominative participle verb "pisteuon" = "pas ho pisteuon"= "everyone who is the believing one" = a noun.

The aoristic present tense presents the action as a simple event or as a present fact without any reference to its progress.

The phrase "should not perish" in John 3:16 is in the aorist tense providing a completed state of never perishing at the moment in the present one becomes the believer.

This is all as a result of the aoristic future tense in both verses of God having so loved the world that He gave His only begotten Son. Since all of the above actions are completed action moments, the aoristic present "whosoever believeth" would be in view if "whosoever believeth" in John 3:16 were in the present tense.

The aorist tense expresses punctiliar action. Indeed the word *aoristos* (aorist) means without limit, unqualified, undefined—which of course is the significance of punctiliar action. Only in the indicative mood (as in both verbs in John 3:16 main clause) does the aorist also indicate past time. It often corresponds to the English perfect (*I have loosed*).

So the aorist tense is viewed as a single, collective whole, a "one-point-in-time" action in which from an external point of view the action is completed—no longer requiring further time to elapse, although it may actually have taken place over a period of time. In the indicative mood the aorist tense denotes action that occurred in the past time, often translated like the English simple past tense.

Notice that "should not perish" is in the aorist tense providing a completed state of never perishing at the moment one becomes the believer. A completed action of never perishing is thus not effected by whether or not the believing continues on after that. Furthermore, a completed action of never perishing is another way of saying one is in a state of having eternal life which immediately follows in parallel in John 3:16 after the connective word, "but," "whosoever believeth in Him should not perish but have eternal life." The two are inseparable, you are never perishing when you have eternal life.

Even in Ephesians 2:8-9 does the Greek tense assure salvation.

For by grace you have been (eimi plus a perfect periphrastic participle) saved in the past with the result that you stand saved forever through faith, and this (salvation) is not from yourselves; it is a gift from God, not of works, lest any man should boast. The Greek perfect periphrastic in Ephesians 2:8 takes the sense of the tense of the participle, indicating the present results of an action completed in the past. This is one of the most emphatic expressions in Greek which indicates there is no possible loss of salvation.

Conclusion. One is not saved and eternally secure by continuous faith but by a moment of faith in Christ.

John 6:35.

And Jesus said unto them, I am the bread of life: he that cometh to me shall never hunger; and he that believeth on me shall never thirst.

Notice in this verse all it takes is one drink (believeth) and one's eternal thirst is forever quenched. This represents the fact that one is eternally saved the moment they believe on Christ, whether they keep believing or stop believing or whether or not they ever believe again.

God bless.

17- OSAS And Suicide.

Many people will disingenuously claim to believe in eternal security but will deny that someone is secure if they commit suicide. They assert that this is the unpardonable sin—the one sin that will cause one to lose their salvation.

But according to the Bible it is not.

Mark 3:28-29.

Verily I say unto you, All sins shall be forgiven unto the sons of men, and blasphemies wherewith soever they shall blaspheme: But he that shall blaspheme against the Holy Ghost hath never forgiveness, but is in danger of eternal damnation.

Suicide is not mentioned here. This sin was a national sin the Pharisees committed and it can't be committed today due to the fact that Jesus is no longer here. Hebrews 1:3. The Bible has many accounts of people committing suicide. Here are a few of them.

Abimelech… (Judges 9:54.)
Saul… (1 Samuel 31:1-4.)
Samson… (Judges 16:28-31.)
Saul's armor-bearer… (1 Samuel 31:5.)
Ahitophel… (2 Samuel 17:23.)
Zimri… (1 Kings 16:18.)
Judas… (Matthew 27:5.)

Now, let's take a look at each account in scripture.

Judges 9:54.

Then he called hastily unto the young man his armourbearer, and said unto him, Draw thy sword, and slay me, that men say not of me, A women slew him. And his young man thrust him through, and he died.

1 Samuel 31:4-6.

Then said Saul unto his armourbearer, Draw thy sword, and thrust me through therewith; lest these uncircumcised come and thrust me through, and abuse me. But his armourbearer would not; for he was sore afraid. Therefore Saul took a sword, and fell upon it. And when his armourbearer saw that Saul was dead, he fell likewise upon his sword, and died with him. So Saul died, and his three sons, and his armourbearer, and all his men, that same day together.

2 Samuel 17:23.

And when Ahithophel saw that his counsel was not followed, he saddled his ass, and arose, and gat him home to his house, to his city, and put his household in order, and hanged himself, and died, and was buried in the sepulchre of his father.

1 Kings 16:18.

And it came to pass, when Zimri saw that the city was taken, that he went into the palace of the king's house, and burnt the king's house over him with fire, and died.

Matthew 27:5.

And he cast down the pieces of silver in the temple, and departed, and went and hanged himself.

Out of all these characters that committed

suicide we can be pretty safe in surmising that that King Saul was saved. 1 Samuel 11:6. Suicide is a horrific sin but all sin is cleansed by the blood of Jesus if one is saved. (1 John 1:7. Titus 2:14. Colossians 2:13.)

When a believer leaves this body they will be in God's presence even if they commit suicide.

2 Corinthians 5:8.

We are confident, I say, and willing rather to be absent from the body, and to be present with the Lord.

Because salvation is based on God's fatherly love, nothing, not even suicide can alter it.

Romans 8:35.

Who shall separate us from the love of Christ? shall tribulation, or distress, or persecution, or famine, or nakedness, or peril, or sword?

Romans 8:38-39.

For I am persuaded, that neither death, nor life, nor angels, nor principalities, nor powers, nor things present, nor things to come, Nor height, nor depth, nor any other creature, shall be able to separate us from the love of God, which is in Christ Jesus our Lord.

Suicide, which is death, can't separate us from God's love and neither can anything else. The truth is believers in Jesus Christ are saved to the uttermost and nothing can change this. NOTHING!

Hebrews 7:25.

Wherefore he is able also to save them to the uttermost that come unto God by him, seeing he ever liveth to make intercession for them.

Conclusion: although suicide is a horrible sin

with many repercussions on loved ones here on earth it cannot keep a believer from heaven. They are eternally secure. (John 6:37.)

God bless.

18 - OSAS And Rewards.

Because eternal life is a free gift, (Romans 6:23, John 4:10,) and Jesus Christ is the guarantor of our entrance into heaven, (John 14:1-3,) the issue of earning eternal rewards is integral. How we live our lives has nothing to do with our salvation, (2 Timothy 1:9, Romans 9:11-16,) but it does have to do with blessings here on earth and future rewards in heaven. Ephesians 1:3, Revelation 2:10.

Before we deal with rewards let's deal with God's chastisement towards His beloved children.

Hebrews 12:6.

For whom the Lord loveth he chasteneth, and scourgeth every son whom he receiveth. If ye endure chastening, God dealeth with you as with sons; for what son is he whom the father chasteneth not? But if ye be without chastisement, whereof all are partakers, then are ye bastards, and not sons. Furthermore we have had fathers of our flesh which corrected us, and we gave them reverence: shall we not much rather be in subjection unto the Father of spirits, and live?

What the heretics that reject eternal security based on how a believer lives have neglected is the simple fact that no one is getting away with anything. Believers in Christ will be disciplined by God as we have seen in the abovementioned verses. They may sin like mad but nothing will go unpunished. We reap what we sow. (Galatians 6:7-

8.)

Aside from the negative aspect of God giving comeuppance where it is duly earned, let's focus on some passages that deal with rewards in heaven, which is the sole reason for serving God in this lifetime.

1 Corinthians 3:11-15.

For other foundation can no man lay than that is laid, which is Jesus Christ. Now if any man build upon this foundation gold, silver, precious stones, wood, hay, stubble; Every man's work shall be made manifest: for the day shall declare it, because it shall be revealed by fire; and the fire shall try every man's work of what sort it is. If any man's work abide which he hath built thereupon, he shall receive a reward. If any man's work shall be burned, he shall suffer loss: but he himself shall be saved; yet so as by fire.

There are three types of rewards that will withstand the symbolic fire of judgment. Gold, silver and precious stone. Living a wasteful life results in works that will be incinerated: namely, wood, hay and stubble. But we also see the person who lived like the devil but still made it to heaven as though by fire. This reinforces the doctrine of eternal security.

2 Corinthians 5:9-10.

Wherefore we labour, that, whether present or absent, we may be accepted of him. For we must all appear before the judgment seat of Christ; that every one may receive the things done in his body, according to that he hath done, whether it be good or bad.

God wants to reward faithful believers. (Matthew 25:21.) That is why He has given us so many things to do in this lifetime.

1—Soul-Winning. Mark 16:15.
2—Praying. 1 Thessalonians 5:17.
3—Bible reading. 1 Timothy 4:13.
4—Giving to the needy. Romans 12:13.
5—Praising God. Psalm 113:1.
6—Attending church. Hebrews 10:25.
7—Fighting against sin. Ephesians 5:3-4.
8—Preaching sermons. 2 Timothy 4:2.
9—Exposing false prophets. Romans 16:17.
10—Communion. Matthew 26:26-29.

The more we do in this lifetime; the more rewards we are going to amass in eternity.

2 Corinthians 9:6.

But this I say, He which soweth sparingly shall reap also sparingly; and he which soweth bountifully shall reap also bountifully.

Conclusion: Salvation is a free gift given to the believer in Christ once and for all. Therefore God wants to reward us based on what we do in this lifetime.

Matthew 5:12.

Rejoice, and be exceeding glad: for great is your reward in heaven: for so persecuted they the prophets which were before you.

The Bible speaks of 5 crowns that believers will receive as rewards. They are.

Incorruptible crown.

It is earned by leading a disciplined life.

1 Corinthians 9:25.

And every man that striveth for the mastery is

temperate in all things. Now they do it to obtain a corruptible crown; but we an incorruptible.

Crown of rejoicing.

It is earned by discipleship and evangelism.
1 Thessalonians 2:19.

For what is our hope, or joy, or crown of rejoicing? Are not even ye in the presence of our Lord Jesus Christ at his coming?

Crown of Glory.

It is earned by shepherding God's flock.
1 Peter 5:4.

And when the chief Shepherd shall appear, ye shall receive a crown of glory that fadeth not away.

Crown of righteousness.

It is earned by loving the Lord's appearing.
2 Timothy 4:8.

Henceforth there is laid up for me a crown of righteousness, which the Lord, the righteous judge, shall give me at that day: and not to me only, but unto all them also that love his appearing.

A carnal Christian who is spiritually asleep will not be receiving this crown. For he clings to the things of this world and is not anticipating the rapture or the second coming of Christ.

Crown of life.

It is earned by enduring trials.
James 1:12.

Blessed is the man that endureth temptation: for when he is tried, he shall receive the crown of life, which the Lord hath promised to them that love him.

Those who struggle in this life will receive this crown. It is not the same as eternal life. One must never confuse the gift of salvation with rewards. The reference in Revelation 2:10 is not as clear as the reference in James for in James says blessed is the man. "Blessings" always pertain to rewards.

2 Samuel 22:21.

The LORD rewarded me according to my righteousness: according to the cleanness of my hands hath he recompensed me.

God bless.

19 - OSAS And Evangelism.

The Bible has much to say about evangelism. Let's look at several verses on this subject.

Proverbs 11:30.

The fruit of the righteous is a tree of life; and he that winneth souls is wise.

Acts 1:8.

But ye shall receive power, after that the Holy Ghost is come upon you: and ye shall be witnesses unto me both in Jerusalem, and in all Judaea, and in Samaria, and unto the uttermost part of the earth.

Mark 16:15.

And he said unto them, Go ye into all the world, and preach the gospel to every creature.

Romans 1:16.

For I am not ashamed of the gospel of Christ: for it is the power of God unto salvation to every one that believeth; to the Jew first, and also to the Greek.

1 Corinthians 9:16.

For though I preach the gospel, I have nothing to glory of: for necessity is laid upon me; yea, woe is unto me, if I preach not the gospel.

1 Corinthians 3:7-9.

So then neither is he that planteth any thing,

neither he that watereth; but God that giveth the increase. Now he that planteth and he that watereth are one: and every man shall receive his own reward according to his own labour. For we are labourers together with God: ye are God's husbandry, ye are God's building.

Evangelism is extremely important and all believers in Christ are commanded to preach the gospel. Titus 1:3. Without the message of eternal security one is not preaching the true gospel and is not evangelizing correctly. It is important that we include it in our gospel presentation. This is the current gospel presentation I use.

****

How To Be Simply Saved.

1. The bad News. We are sinners. (Romans 3:23.) We deserve to be punished in hell for our sins.

2. The Good News. Jesus Christ who is God's Son died on the cross for all of your sins. He was buried & rose again to give you eternal life in heaven as a free gift. (1 Corinthians 15:3-4. Romans 6:23.)

3. How am I saved?
Believe on the Lord Jesus Christ and thou shalt be saved. (Acts 16:31.)

4. Once saved, always saved.
Jesus said in John 6:47. Verily, verily, I say unto you, He that believeth on me hath everlasting life.

Do you believe that you are saved by grace and promised heaven because Jesus died for you?
Yes_ No_.

Here are some tips for evangelism.
1. Make the gospel as simple and accessible as possible. John 3:16. Free grace. Faith alone. No works. Keep the handout short and sweet. I have had people ask me how to be saved (long time ago) and I handed them a tract with three pages of gospel literature and then the asker frowned

because of all the laborious reading. Keep it real short.

    Example. You are a sinner. Jesus Christ died for your sins, was buried and rose again. John 3:16, Acts 16:31. You can fill in the explanatory rifts with more information as you engage dialogically.

    2. Have many types of handouts and plenty. Some people, due to false religion are being indoctrinated to repudiate certain symbolic icons. So we need to be diverse in our handout repertoire. Crosses, coins, tickets to heaven, tracts, fliers… etc.

    3. Ask people if they know for sure where they would go if they were to die today. To heaven or to hell. If they say they don't know ask them if you can show them either with the Bible or some verses on a tract or flier. This of course is something you build into the conversation and not something for the introduction. If they say they don't care or act indifferent explain the reality of John 3:36.

    4. Dress cordially, smell fresh, use cologne, body spray and breath-mints to optimize personal hygiene. Leave no room for assumed hypocrisy-- lost people are natural "hypocrite hunters." They will look for tattoos, foul-language and other marks of hypocrisy. Be careful who you hobnob with as you witness to people. Guilt by association is very prevalent.

    5. Go in couples if possible. Even if one person is a silent partner. There is a power in numbers. Deuteronomy 19:15.

    6. Pray heavily before Soul-Winning. 1 Thessalonians 5:17.

7. Have a positive attitude. The non-soul-winner has a defeatist attitude and that stymies their evangelistic outcome.

8. Practice evangelizing in a classroom setting with other believers to get accustomed to dialogically speaking with strangers.

9. Never assume someone is saved or even lost for that matter. Keep it an open playing field. Never assume someone is too young to be saved or understand the gospel. Matthew 18:6.

10. Always use KJV Bible verses and never fail to explain eternal security. Once saved, always saved. John 6:37-40.

11. Don't be in a hurry to stop soul-winning. Avoid a time constraint.

12. Have many simple gospel verses memorized. John 3:15, 16, 18, 36, 5:24, 6:47.

13. Leave gospel material behind if nobody is home and also if they say "we're not interested" and won't let you talk to them.

14. 1 John 1:9. Sin hinders soul-winning. We should confess sin continually.

15. Always ask if you can give others in the household some free handouts. I usually use crosses or coins containing a solid gospel verse.

Here is an effective evangelistic method from my previous book on Soul-Winning entitled: Hand-evangelism.

Use non-permanent markers and use black-SIN, brown-cross, and red-blood.

One can tell others about the Good News of our Saviour Jesus Christ, who saves and gives eternal life as a free gift to all who simply believe in Him for it.

—Step one: draw a cross on the inside of your thumb. Representing Jesus Christ who died for all sinners.

—Step two: Write out on the inside of your fingers S.I.N.S. Denoting that we are all sinners. Romans 3:23.

—Step three: On the backside of your hand write out B.L.O.O.D. beneath your knuckles.

Above the D on the back of your thumb draw a horizontal plane and then atop… an arrow pointing upward to the heavens.

To present this show your inner thumb and the cross and explain the death, burial and resurrection of Christ. Then wiggle your other fingers to show people/sinners. Then go over the Gospel. Lower your thumb to explain the death, lower it even more to explain the burial and then explain that we are buried with Him in baptism (Romans 6:4.) by closing your entire fist.

Now show the back of the thumb as it ascends. The D stands for "death" and the arrow represents the fact that believers are going to heaven having been raised again with Christ. (Colossians 3:1-4. 2 Corinthians 4:14.)

Now show the back of your fingers erected high wherein is the word: B.L.O.O.D. Explain that as saved people: all of our sins (past, present and future) have been washed away by the precious blood of Jesus. 1 John 1:7, Ephesians 1:7, 1 Peter

1:18-19. Isaiah 1:18. Never to be seen again. Isaiah 38:17.

Finish it off with a simple salvation verse: Let the listener know that because Jesus did all of this for them He has promised eternal life that can never be lost if they will believe on Him for it.

John 6:47.

Verily, verily, I say unto you he that believeth on me hath everlasting life.

Conclusion: Only those who are mulishly sold out on the doctrine of eternal security can do any veridical evangelizing. We know we have eternal life. 1 John 5:13. And we also know that anyone else who believes in Jesus has everlasting life and will be raised up at the last day as well. John 6:40. God holds all His children in His hands forevermore. (Deuteronomy 33:3.) The message of eternal security is what all sinners need to hear.

John 6:35.

And Jesus said unto them, I am the bread of life: he that cometh to me shall never hunger; and he that believeth on me shall never thirst.

God bless.

20 - OSAS And Church History.

Some of the opponents of eternal security like to claim that the early church fathers through their patristic writings denied eternal security and even salvation by grace through faith alone. (Sola Fide.)

The reason they say this is to make eternal security seem like a new-fangled and erroneous idea in order to refute it with history on their side. But if you do your homework on this subject, you will find actual documentations of the early church fathers affirming eternal security by faith alone in Christ alone.

Here is a random list of some of the patristic quotes that affirm that many of the early church fathers believed in eternal salvation at the moment of belief in Christ.

1. Clement of Rome.

"And we, therefore are not justified of ourselves or by our wisdom or insight or religious devotion or the holy deeds we have done from the heart, but by that faith by which almighty God has justified all men from the very beginning."

2. Tertullian.

"Grant that, in days gone by, there was salvation by means of bare faith, before the passion and resurrection of the Lord."

3. Origen.
"The apostles saith, that the justification onely of faith sufficeth."

4. Justin Martyr.
"For Abraham was declared by God to be righteous, not on account of circumcision, but on account of faith."

5. Julian of Toledo.
"The righteousness of faith by which we are justified... that we believe in him whom we do not see, and that, being cleansed by faith, we shall eventually see him in whom we now believe. If someone believes in Christ... he can be saved by faith alone."

6. Ambrose.
"God chose that man should seek salvation by faith rather than by works, lest anyone should glory in his deeds and thereby incur sin."
"Without the works of the Law to an ungodly man, that is to say, a Gentile, believing in Christ, his 'faith is imputed for righteousness,' as also it was to Abraham. How, then, can the Jews imagine, that through the works of the Law they are justified with the justification of Abraham, when they see that Abraham was justified, not by the works of the Law, but by faith alone? There is no need, therefore, of the Law, since through faith alone, an ungodly man is justified with God."

7. Augustine.

"Righteousness is not by the law, but by faith, and is the gift of God by Jesus Christ." "When I shall be just, it is Thy justice, because I am just by that justice which is given me of Thee, for I believe in Him that justifieth the wicked, that my faith may be deputed for righteousness."

8. Ignatius.

"To me, Christ is in the place of all ancient muniments. For His Cross, and His death, and His resurrection, and the faith which is through Him, are my unpolluted muniments; and in these, through your prayers, I am willing to have been justified."

9. Polycarp.

"The Lord Jesus Christ, who endured to submit unto death for our sins; whom God raised up, having loosed the pains of hell; in whom ye believe, not having seen Him, but believing ye rejoice with joy unspeakable and full of glory.... knowing that through grace ye are saved, not of works, but by the will of God, through Jesus Christ."

10. Irenius.

"No one, indeed while placed out of reach of our Lord's benefits, has power to procure for himself the means of salvation."

Conclusion. Despite what many skeptics of

eternal security say it has always been taught and as long the children of God are being truthful to God's word it will always be taught henceforth and forevermore.

1 Peter 1:23-25.

Being born again, not of corruptible seed, but of incorruptible, by the word of God, which liveth and abideth for ever. For all flesh is as grass, and all the glory of man as the flower of grass. The grass withereth, and the flower thereof falleth away: But the word of the Lord endureth for ever. And this is the word which by the gospel is preached unto you.

God bless.

21- OSAS In The Old Testament.

We see eternal security clearly in the New Testament but is this teaching found in the Old Testament as well?

The author of Hebrews made it clear that believer in Christ are eternally secure.

Hebrews 10:10-14.

By the which will we are sanctified through the offering of the body of Jesus Christ once for all. And every priest standeth daily ministering and offering oftentimes the same sacrifices, which can never take away sins: But this man, after he had offered one sacrifice for sins for ever, sat down on the right hand of God; From henceforth expecting till his enemies be made his footstool. For by one offering he hath perfected for ever them that are sanctified.

However some theologians believed that the OT believers were not secure. I hope to explain how and why that is wrong. Hebrews 13:8.

Eternal security is what makes Christianity distinct from other religions. It's what makes the gospel good news (glad tidings, Luke 1:19.) If we weren't secure in Christ, this book would be pointless, but so would life and our Christian walk!

The reason for this subset is to show you that eternal security is consistent in the Bible and it can be found in the Old Testament as well as the New Testament.

I've devoted this subset in declaring the security we have in Christ based on the Old Testament promises.

First of all David the Psalmist had full security in God, security that God would not fail him and that salvation was certain. Could he have used such language had he felt otherwise?

O give thanks unto the LORD; for he is good; for his mercy endureth for ever.

O LORD, there is none like thee, neither is there any God beside thee, according to all that we have heard with our ears. (1 Chronicles 16:34, 17:20).

He knew that salvation wasn't something that constantly hung in the balance like an active pendulum. Salvation wasn't a fickle or fluctuant thing. The Bible uses pretty strong language when it describes salvation.

1 Chronicles 16:17.

And hath confirmed the same to Jacob for a law, and to Israel for an everlasting covenant.

Sounds pretty secure.

Psalm 125:2.

As the mountains are round about Jerusalem, so the LORD is round about his people from henceforth even for ever.

Psalm 37:28-29.

For the LORD loveth judgment, and forsaketh not his saints; they are preserved for ever: but the seed of the wicked shall be cut off. The righteous shall inherit the land, and dwell therein for ever.

These verses in the Old Testament prove that we are perfectly secure in Christ.
The doctrine of eternal security is essential to understanding everything else about the Bible. Here are some more OT verses that prove that we are secure in Christ.

Psalm 37:23-24.

The steps of a good man are ordered by the LORD: and he delighteth in his way. Though he fall, he shall not be utterly cast down: for the LORD upholdeth him with his hand.

I used these verses to disprove the doctrine of perseverance of the saints and my emphasis was on Israel and their lack of obedience. Look at these verses again with the emphasis this time on God's immutable promises.

Psalms 89:29-34.

His seed also will I make to endure for ever, and his throne as the days of heaven. If his children forsake my law, and walk not in my judgments; If they break my statutes, and keep not my commandments; Then will I visit their transgression with the rod, and their iniquity with stripes. Nevertheless <u>my loving kindness will I not utterly take from him</u>, nor suffer my <u>faithfulness to fail</u>. My covenant will <u>I not break</u>, nor alter the thing that is gone out of my lips. Once have I sworn by my holiness that I will not lie unto David.

The Old Testament is replete with verses on security.

Genesis 17:7.

And I will establish my covenant between me

and thee and thy seed after thee in their generations for an everlasting covenant, to be a God unto thee, and to thy seed after thee.

Psalm 41:13.
Blessed be the LORD God of Israel from everlasting, and to everlasting. Amen, and Amen.

Isaiah 45:17.
But Israel shall be saved in the LORD with an everlasting salvation: ye shall not be ashamed nor confounded world without end.

Genesis 9:16.
And the bow shall be in the cloud; and I will look upon it, that I may remember the everlasting covenant between God and every living creature of all flesh that is upon the earth.

Genesis 48:4.
And said unto me, Behold, I will make thee fruitful, and multiply thee, and I will make of thee a multitude of people; and will give this land to thy seed after thee for an everlasting possession.

1 Chronicles 16:17.
And hath confirmed the same to Jacob for a law, and to Israel for an everlasting covenant.

There are some verses in both the OT and NT that when the word 'salvation' or *teshuah,* are used are not referring to eternal salvation. *Teshuah* in Hebrew refers to just physical deliverance or being rescued from dire circumstances, but the Isaiah 45:17 reference is obviously about eternal salvation for it clearly says everlasting salvation. This is a promise of security. Temporal salvation is obviously not eternal. Eternal salvation obviously is!

Ezekiel 16:60.

Nevertheless I will remember my covenant with thee in the days of thy youth, and I will establish unto thee an everlasting covenant.

Daniel 9:24.

Seventy weeks are determined upon thy people and upon thy holy city, to finish the transgression, and to make an end of sins, and to make reconciliation for iniquity, and to bring in everlasting righteousness, and to seal up the vision and prophecy, and to anoint the most Holy.

God bless.

22 - How To Defend Eternal Security.

When people combat or try to confute this doctrine it is because they have rejected God's clear word and are quite nescient when it comes to biblical and theological subjects. The primary causal culprit is religion. From religion we get tradition. Tradition always disallows one to believe the Bible and in turn causes one to outright reject the clear teachings of scripture.

Mark 7:6-13.

He answered and said unto them, Well hath Esaias prophesied of you hypocrites, as it is written, This people honoureth me with their lips, but their heart is far from me. Howbeit in vain do they worship me, teaching for doctrines the commandments of men. For laying aside the commandment of God, ye hold the tradition of men, as the washing of pots and cups: and many other such like things ye do. And he said unto them, Full well ye reject the commandment of God, that ye may keep your own tradition. For Moses said, Honour thy father and thy mother; and, Whoso curseth father or mother, let him die the death: But ye say, If a man shall say to his father or mother, It is Corban, that is to say, a gift, by whatsoever thou mightest be profited by me; he shall be free. And ye suffer him no more to do ought for his father or *his mother; <u>Making the word of God of none effect through your tradition</u>, which ye have delivered: and many such like things do ye.*

We must let people know that the reason they don't believe OSAS is because they don't believe the Bible and rather hold to their man-made tradition instead. Fallible man is the one that came up with the idea that salvation can be lost or that it is somehow not secure.

Natural man actually. 1 Corinthians 2:12-14.
We need to challenge them with:
What would cause salvific loss?
One sin, tens sins, a hundred sins?
And then ask them if they sin.
Or have they lost their salvation or not.

Sadly, most people that reject eternal security aren't saved and won't get saved and are thus reprobates. (2 Timothy 2:7-8.) However there is still hope for some. Some will reject the Arminian heresy if they see enough clear verses disproving it.

Another thing we must address is the issue of them not knowing what "eternal" or "everlasting" (life) means. Most won't want to admit this but this is true. Anyone who thinks salvation can be lost or forfeited doesn't even know what these basic words mean.

Next. Anyone who disbelieves eternal security is patently calling God a liar. John 11:26, 1 John 5:9-13. It may be helpful if they would admit that.

Here are a list of problems one faces if they

believe salvation can be lost.

1. It renders God a liar. 1 John 5:10.

2. It makes assurance impossible. 1 John 5:13.

3. Suicide right after conversion would be advisable.

4. We would live in constant fear. 1 John 4:18.

5. Salvation would be based on works. Titus 3:5.

6. Christ didn't finished anything at the cross. John 19:30.

7. It is another Jesus. 2 Corinthians 11:1-5.

8. Everlasting would really mean temporary. John 17:3-4.

9. John 3:16 would not be true.

10. Losing salvation is not good news. Luke 2:10.

If one opposes eternal security they must deal with all these points. Defending eternal security is simple. Point someone to the scripture and challenge them to believe it. John 10:28. God is not a deceiver, traitor or Indian giver. When He promises eternal life; He keeps His promise. Romans 11:29. 1 John 2:25. That is the crux of eternal security. Anyone who is saved should naturally believe that they will always be saved.

When one doesn't embrace eternal security it could be that they are not saved at all and need to get saved.

Acts 16:31 doesn't say: Believe on the Lord Jesus Christ and thou shalt be *temporarily safe*, no it says saved and saved has a "D" at the end— denoting that salvation is done. When we are saved by the grace of God, we are saved once and for all. Once saved, always saved.

One of the best ways to defend eternal security is to explain that man would have to undo everything God has done at the point of salvation.

There are forty things that have transpired at the moment one believes on Christ for salvation. These things are irreversible and none of them can ever be undone. Here is a list of them.

1.) Access to God. (Romans 5:2.)
2.) The Baptism of the Holy Spirit. (1 Corinthians 12:13.)
3.) The Unique Availability of Divine Power. (Ephesians 6:10.)
4.) Efficacious Grace. (Ephesians 2:8-9.)
5.) Election. (Ephesians1:3-4.)
6.) Equal Privilege and Opportunity. (Galatians 3:26-28.)
7.) Escrow Blessings. (Ephesians 1:3.)
8.) Reception of Eternal Life. (1 John 5:11-13.)
9.) Eternal Security. (John 10:28-29.)
10.) The filling of the Holy Spirit. (Ephesians 5:18.)
11.) A Secure, Immovable Foundation. (Deuteronomy 32:4.)
12.) Being presented as a gift from God the Father to God the Son. (John 10:29.)
13.) Deliverance from the Great White Throne Judgment and the Lake of Fire. (John 3:18.)
14.) Identification with God the Son in Biblical Analogy. (1 Corinthians 15:45.)

15.) The Indwelling of God the Father. (John 14:22-23.)
16) The Indwelling of God the Holy Spirit. (Romans 8:11.)
17.) The Indwelling of God the Son. (John 14:20.)
18.) An Eternal Inheritance. (Hebrews 9:15.)
19.) Justification. (Galatians 2:16.)
20.) Transference into the Kingdom of God. (Ephesians 2:3.)
21.) Deliverance from the Kingdom of Satan. (Colossians 1:13.)
22.) The New Spiritual Species. (2 Corinthians 5:17.)
23.) Positional Sanctification—adopted as Adult sons. (Romans 8:15.)
24.) Predestination. (Ephesians 1:5.)
25.) Born again. (John 3:3-7.)
26.) Propitiation. (Romans 3:24-25.)
27.) The Unique Predesigned Plan of God for the Church-age. (Galatians 5:16.)
28.) Reconciliation. (2 Corinthians 5:19.)
29.) Redemption. (Ephesians. 1:7.)
30.) Regeneration. (Titus 3:5.)
31.) The guarantee of a Resurrection Body. (John 11:25-26.)
32.) The Imputed Righteousness of God. (Romans 3:22.)
33.) The Royal Ambassadorship. (2 Corinthians 5:20.)
34.) Entrance into the Royal Family of God. (Revelation 1:6.)
35.) The Royal Priesthood. (1 Peter 2:5.)

36.) The Removal of all Scar Tissue from the Soul. (Isaiah 43:25.)
37.) The Sealing Ministry of the Holy Spirit. (Ephesians 1:13-14.)
38.) Deliverance from the Power and Influence of the Old Sin Nature. (Romans 2:29.)
39.) The Distribution of Spiritual Gifts. (1 Corinthians 12:7-11.)
40.) The Unlimited Atonement. (2 Corinthians 5:14-15.)
God bless.

Addendum.

Eternal security has been one of my favorite things to preach on and write about. It is the one doctrine that one can't afford to be wrong about. It is also one of the doctrines Satan has hid from the lost: 2 Corinthians 4:3-4. He uses anything from backsliders to faith-changers to people that claim to be Christians but give biometric indications that they are not. But this is all empirical reasoning considering that one's eternal fate is based on God's Word and nothing else. (John 17:17.)

That is why we must mulishly contend for the truth on this salient subject. One way to assure that people believe this doctrine is a simple gospel quiz. A quiz should start off with a clear presentation of the gospel followed by a bunch of pertinent questions.

Here is an eternal security quiz.

God sent His Son, Jesus Christ to die on the cross for your sins. He was buried and rose again to save you from hell and give you the gift of eternal life.

John 3:36a.
He that believeth on the Son hath everlasting life.

1. Do you believe that you are saved and going to heaven because Jesus died for you?
A. Yes.
B. No.
C. Unsure.
2. How many people did Jesus die for?
A. All.
B. Some.
C. The elect.
3. How many sins did Jesus died for?
A. Only past sins.
B. Some.
C. All.
4. How many times do you have to get saved?
A. One.
B. Two.
C. Seven.
5. Is eternal life a gift or is it based on works?
A. It based on works.
B. A free gift.
C. Both.
6. If a saved person lives in sin where will he go?
A. Hell.
B. Heaven.
C. Purgatory.
6. If a believer stops believing where will he go?
A. Heaven.
B. Hell.
C. Unsure.

8. **Do you have to repent of your sins to be saved?**
A. No. Just believe.
B. Yes.
C. Sometimes.

9. **Is believing in Jesus enough to be saved?**
A. Yes.
B. No.
C. You must keep believing.

10. **Can we know for sure we will go to heaven?**
A. No.
B. Maybe.
C. Yes.

The answers.

1—it depends on what they say.	John 3:36.
2—A. All.	1 John 2:2.
3—C. All.	1 John 1:7.
4—A. One.	John 6:37.
5—B. A free gift.	Romans 6:23.
6—B. Heaven.	John 10:28.
7—A. Heaven.	2 Timothy 2:13.
8—A. No. Just believe.	Acts 16:31.
9—A. Yes.	John 6:47.
10—C. Yes.	1 John 5:13.

My Doctrinal Beliefs.

I hope you enjoyed the previous subsets. But in case you are wondering what I believe in other areas concerning the Bible and biblical doctrine. This sums it up.

What I believe…

***I believe in the verbal and plenary inspiration of the Bible (KJV), that the Bible is the infallible and inerrant Word of God, and the exclusive and sufficient guide for salvation, doctrine, and the spiritual life of the believer. 2 Timothy 3:16-17; 2 Peter 1:20-21.

***I believe in the Trinity, and their triune co-equality. Matthew 28:19. 1 John 5:7.

***I believe in the finished work of Jesus Christ on the cross as the unique, once and for all sacrifice for the personal sins of mankind. John 3:16 & 36; 2 Corinthians 5:21. John 19:30.

***I believe that a person receives eternal salvation by a singular moment of faith alone in Christ alone. Acts 4:12 Romans 4:5, Luke 8:50.

***I believe in eternal salvation and eternal security - "once saved, always saved." John 10:28-29. John 3:15. John 5:24.

***I believe in the universal indwelling of the Holy Spirit in every believer at the moment of salvation. 1 Corinthians 6:19. Romans 8:9.

***I believe in the sinfulness of man and his need for the personal Saviour, Jesus Christ. Acts 26:18. Ecclesiastes 7:20. Acts 16:31.

***I believe in the bodily resurrection of Jesus Christ from the grave. 1 Corinthians 15:20. John

11:25-26.

***I believe that we are in the dispensation of grace: the Church Age, and are believer-priests. 1 Peter 2:5-9.

***I believe in the pretribulation rapture. 1 Thessalonians 4:13.

***I believe in communion, prayer, Christian fellowship, and the teaching of sound doctrine. Not as requirements for salvation but because one is saved by grace and desires to grow spiritually. Acts 2:42.

***I believe in separation from those sectarian groups, churches, and organizations which violate or teach against sound Biblical doctrines. Romans 16:17.

***I believe in a literal hell that all rejecters of Christ will suffer in for all eternity.

***I reject: Calvinism in any form. Arminianism, Lordship/repentance Salvation. Catholicism, Mormonism and any other cultic religion.

Those are my basic doctrinal beliefs. Now an ancillary and personal belief I hold to is that all born-again believers in Jesus Christ should be avid and incessant soul-winners thus boldly proclaiming the gospel of grace to all people. Mark 16:15. 1 Corinthians 15:3-4. John 6:47.

God bless.

JESUS
A
V
E
S

Made in the USA
Middletown, DE
15 June 2020